Successful hunters

SENECA RAY STODDARD

Versatile Camera-Artist

By

MAITLAND C. DE SORMO

Adirondack Yesteryears Inc.
Drawer 209
Saranac Lake, N. Y. 12983

Other books written or edited by same author:

Told Around the Campfire (van Hoevenbergh Story)

Noah John Rondeau, Adirondack Hermit

Adirondack French Louie (Reprinter)

Old Times in the Adirondacks

ISBN 978-0-96011-581-5

Printed in United States of America
By The George Little Press, Burlington, Vermont

Library of Congress Catalog Card Number 72-905866

Dedication

To Pauline S. Smith of Glens Falls, long-time friend and Adirondack enthusiast, who first brought to my attention the importance and location of the incomparable Stoddard collection. Her insistence, persistence and downright determination provided the prodding which finally ended with the publication of this long-overdue big book about a really big and gifted man.

Table of Contents

List of Illustrations

Adirondack Miscellany

Introduction

by

Robert F. Hall, Editor, The Conservationist

It almost never fails — those who come under the spell of the Adirondacks develop an insatiable appetite for knowledge of the region's past. To identify with these wooded hills and running streams in the present, it seems, is not enough. The confirmed Adirondack buff is a haunter of such archives as we have: several museums, many libraries and the dusty files of our weekly newspapers.

Maitland De Sormo thus had a ready-made public for the historical works which he has written, edited or published since he retired as a teacher down-state and came to live year-round in Saranac Lake. He has served that public well, not only in the quality of the books and articles on Adirondack subjects which he has made available to the rest of us, but in his uncanny faculty for locating and uncovering memorabilia of this region's past.

Until Mait De Sormo walked into my editorial office in Warrensburg in the autumn of 1963, my notion of an Adirondack photographer began and ended with Matthew Brady. Mait made me aware of Brady's distinguished successor, Seneca Ray Stoddard, a Glens Falls boy who made good first by his photography, his maps and his writing on the Adirondacks and subsequently by unusual and dramatic pictures in many parts of the world. From a large cardboard box Mait brought out dozens of photographs of Adirondack landscapes, resort hotels from Saratoga to Paul Smith's, steamboats plying our larger lakes and portraits of such legendary guides as Old Mountain Phelps, Alvah Dunning, Bill Nye and Mitchell Sabattis.

In *Adirondack Life,* which at the time was a magazine supplement to the Warrensburg-Lake George *News,* I published Maitland De Sormo's article on Stoddard, illustrated with many of these pictures. For most of the present generation of Adirondackers, as for me, this was a first introduction to a talented man who deserved something better than the oblivion to which he had been consigned.

What De Sormo has done, however, is not only to rescue the forgotten works of Stoddard but to acquaint us with the personality of the man.

11

Widely read, he was, it is now clear, a person of vast talents, witty, attractive; one whose companionship would be valued both in town and in the wilds. His 130-page narrative of his 1873 trip by boat, stage and foot through the Adirondack wilderness, which De Sormo recently made available in a new edition of *Old Times in the Adirondacks* is informative and entertaining. His style of humorous exaggeration of the difficulties of the journey, and his abundant use of earthy anecdotes picked up along the way, reminded me of Mark Twain's *Roughing It* which appeared almost simultaneously.

Among Adirondackers hard put to wrest a livelihood from these granite hills and sparsely-populated valleys, only a few are relieved of the necessity of catering to the tourists. It is true today and it was no less true in Stoddard's time. With energy, foresight and a canny business instinct, Stoddard as a young man made for himself a career in that industry. His photographs of resort hotels and steamboats, prized now for their accurate portrayal of the lifestyle of the wealthy visitors of a century ago, were made for guidebooks — *Adirondacks Illustrated* and *Lake George and Lake Champlain Guide* — which Stoddard produced at a profit, revising each year to keep his advertisers happy. He was equally expert as a map maker, artist and finally as an editor and publisher. His magazine, *The Northern Monthly,* enabled him to combine all these talents with that of an accomplished writer.

Of his literary work, I remember especially his article on the Pottersville Fair, an amusing vignette of our homespun ancestors enjoying a rowdy good time.

If this isn't enough, Stoddard was also an innovator and inventor and apparently was one of the first to devise a superior method for night photography. His magnesium flares produced impressive pictures of the Statue of Liberty, the Washington Square Arch in New York city, the Arc de Triomphe in Paris, and more to our taste, several of surveyors, hunters, guides and hotel guests in lean-tos facing Adirondack campfires.

Maitland De Sormo is an impassioned partisan of Stoddard, but that should not surprise us. Columbus felt strongly about the new world he had discovered and Boswell defended every idiosyncracy of Samuel Johnson. Moreover, De Sormo resents deeply the cavalier treatment or the complete absence of treatment of Stoddard by later historians of the Adirondacks. If De Sormo is similarly neglected by historians of this era, I would resent that.

Willsboro, New York
April 1972

Seneca Ray Stoddard, Versatile Camera-Artist

Preface

There were four nearly equally compelling reasons why I finally decided to write the biography of the versatile, incredibly industrious Seneca Ray Stoddard. Undoubtedly, the primary motivating factor was my discovery some years ago that practically every reasonably well-informed Upstate New Yorker knew surprisingly little about a man who, at the height of his career, was every bit as renowned as Murray and Colvin and whose total contribution to the Adirondack region was demonstrably greater and more varied.

Three generations ago (1880-1910) his superb photography, excellent maps, best-selling guidebooks, hard-hitting editorials, and crowd-pleasing illustrated lectures played a very important part in the eventual creation of the Adirondack Park, as well as in acquainting the nation with the magnificent natural scenic and recreational appeal provided by our much-loved mountains.

For decades, however, his name and work seemed relatively unknown. Moreover, and even more ironical, he was almost invariably confused with his distinguished distant cousin and close contemporary — John L. Stoddard — who was unquestionably the most successful lecturer of his time but not a photographer or artist.

The third and undeniably the strongest factor which influenced my decision was the somewhat surprisingly brief coverage accorded Stoddard by the late Alfred L. Donaldson in his highly-rated two-volume *History of the Adirondacks*. In this work the esteemed historian devoted an entire eulogistic chapter to the youthful Harry Radford but relegated Stoddard to footnote status and even then gave 1918 rather than 1917 as the correct year of his death.

Moreover, in comparing Radford's *Woods and Waters,* a quarterly, with Stoddard's *Northern Monthly,* Donaldson downgraded the latter periodical because its content matter did not deal exclusively with Adirondack material. A careful analysis of Radford's much smaller publication shows even fewer articles on this area along with a disproportionately larger advertising section.

Another example of Donaldson's oversight can be found in Volume II, page 200 of his landmark history of the region. While citing Martin V. B. Ives' *Through the Adirondacks in Eighteen Days* for being "an altogether entertaining contribution to Adirondack lore," he did mention the many excellent and unusual photographs; but even though Stoddard's name appears under nine of these and an additional thirty-six were also his work, the historian neglected to give him the customary credit.

In fairness to Donaldson and with due respect for his impressive achievement in spite of rapidly declining health, it can logically be assumed that he was either unaware or uninformed about Stoddard's total contribution and career. But since Donaldson was and is the most comprehensive historian of the Adirondacks, it is therefore regrettably necessary that such critical comments be registered in order to set the record straight.

Nor was lack of recognition of Stoddard's importance limited solely to historians. Several years ago Howard Mason, the sage of Cleverdale on Lake George, told me that after the famed photographer's death and the subsequent housecleaning operations, he had personally seen several loads of the larger (10″ x 12″ up to 18″ x 22″) glass negatives (wet plates) hauled away by a Glens Falls florist to be first cleaned and then used to replace broken panes on his greenhouse!

Even more incredible but nevertheless true was Mason's remark that some of the same type plates had also been deliberately smashed and then tossed between partitions of an old camp for insulation purposes!

The fourth and final reason for the publication of this book was my acquisition of the extensive Stoddard collection. By great good fortune and the notably generous cooperation of some of his relatives, I am now the custodian of the residue of a remarkable career. This trove included several thousand photographs, wet plates and paper negatives, guidebooks, maps and original map sketches, some 30 oil, water color and pen and ink drawings, proof albums, ledgers and account books, part of his personal library, unpublished manuscripts, press clippings, correspondence and other memorabilia.

Therefore, as the owner of so much of the lifetime work of this extraordinarily talented man, I consider it a responsibility tantamount to an out and out obligation to do everything possible not only to revive but to perpetuate his fame.

Furthermore, I have also managed to arrange it so that at least a representative number of his photographs have been acquired by organizations, libraries, museums and collectors in the areas in which they were originally taken. This, I believe, is as it should be and I have derived an appreciable amount of self-satisfaction from carrying out this aspect of what has become a sort of mission.

Another means of paying tribute to his memory has been a series of articles either about him or featuring his material. These have appeared in

Adirondack Life[1], *North Country Life* and its successor — *York State Tradition, New York Folklore Quarterly, Portfolio* and *Down East Magazine*. Illustrated lectures, radio and TV programs throughout the North Country and elsewhere have also helped to further the project.

By actual last count one hundred 19th century authors and agencies plus at least 25 recent writers have used Stoddard photos to enhance their own literary efforts. In most instances the users credited the source but in far too many cases — especially in the early days — the customary captions were either cropped or else the names of the engraving firms were substituted. Nowadays the work is becoming so well-known that the immediate reaction to one of his characteristic products is "That's a Stoddard."

Particularly gratifying to me has been the very favorable reception given a less-known phase of his versatility — his painting. Originally part of the main collection some of these are now owned by the Adirondack Museum at Blue Mountain Lake, and by other discerning collectors.

Needless to say, I would not have been able to make much more than the proverbial dent in the desired agenda without the wholehearted cooperation of quite a few people. Foremost among these have been the late Hiram and Bertha (Birdie) Stoddard, nephew of S. R., and his wife; and Ernestine, their daughter. Their enthusiasm — Birdie's especially — eagerness and generosity were both unforgettable and unforgotten.

Robert Hall, former editor and publisher of the Warrensburg-Lake George *News* and its supplement *Adirondack Life* and present editor of the New York State *Conservationist*, has also been of considerable service. By printing the Stoddard articles and featuring his photos at other times, Bob has done a great deal to help rekindle Stoddard's fame.

Glyndon Cole, publisher of *York State Tradition* and head of the New York State Collection of Feinberg Memorial Library of State University College in Plattsburgh, has long been impressed by Stoddard's incomparable camera skill and has used many pictures for illustration in his magazine.

Those cited represent but the outstanding few among many who have made it possible for me to do as much as I have in the pursuit of this challenging but eminently gratifying personal project.

---

1.   Former supplement to Warrensburg-Lake George *News*.

Chapter 1

Stoddard's Ancestry And Early Years

According to the Stoddard family history the first of that name to become prominent was William Stoddard, or de la Standard as the name was then written. A Norman knight he was a standard bearer for his cousin, William the Conqueror, and accompanied him on the invasion of England in 1066. When that country was redistributed among the victors, Stoddard was granted extensive holdings near Elthem, Kent, some seven miles from London Bridge, and thereby became one of the landed and titled gentry.

It is a matter of record that 400 acres of this estate were still owned by his descendants in 1490 and remained theirs until the death of Nicholas Stoddard, a bachelor, in 1765.

In 1639 Anthony, another in William's lineage, decided that life under the Stuart kings was no longer tolerable. Archbishop Laud, acting on orders from Charles I, was mercilessly imposing upon many of his unwilling subjects a form of worship which was indistinguishable from Catholicism. Being a staunch, outspoken Protestant, Anthony refused to comply and, rather than endure the inevitable persecution, decided to emigrate to America.

In making this difficult decision Stoddard knew that he and his family were giving up a life of comfort and social distinction. His wife, Mary, was the sister of Sir George Downing, who later became Lord of the Exchequer and after whom Downing Street in London was named, and the niece of Gov. Winthrop.

Once the decision had been made, however, there was very little delay before Stoddard, his wife and their three sons sailed for Boston and a new life as linen merchant in that community of about a thousand inhabitants. Recognition of Anthony's character and ability were not long in coming because he was admitted a Freeman in 1640, was elected a representative in 1650, 1659 and 1660. Moreover, he was annually returned to that office during the twenty consecutive years from 1665 to 1684.

Directly across the Charles River, in a village later named Cambridge, the first college in America had been founded just three years previously.

At that time the general court of the colony had established a fund of 400 pounds for the purpose of building a "school or college" to educate English and Indian youths.

When John Harvard, the eminent Puritan minister, died during that same year (1639), he left half his estate — some 780 pounds and 260 books —to the new seat of learning in the wilderness which, most appropriately, was named after him.

Solomon, oldest son of Anthony Stoddard, was graduated from this college in 1662 and became its first librarian (1667 to 1674). Apparently he was also the first Stoddard to display the intellectual prowess which later characterized a remarkable number of the succeeding generations of this family. As evidence of this renown, by 1750 six more bearers of that name had also been graduated from the same establishment.

Another pronounced trait of the Stoddards was their religious ardor, a zeal which had brought the first Anthony to the New World. Many of the men became ministers and most of the others became very active in the work of their churches. Outstanding among these worthies were Jonathan Edwards and Cotton Mather, reputedly the most eloquent preachers in colonial New England. Edwards, who was considered to be the possessor of the greatest intellect of his time, was the nephew and successor of Solomon Stoddard, minister at Northhampton for several years after his service as librarian at Harvard.

Other notable descendants of the first Anthony in America were the Sherman brothers — John, for many years senator from Ohio and William T., one of the great generals and strategists of the Civil War.

Anthony II, one of the sons of Solomon, also a minister and Harvard graduate, was a man of more than ordinary talents. In addition to a formidable knowledge of the law he also understood medicine and practiced curing the bodies as well as the souls of his extensive parish. He was no weakling but a militant Christian. Besides his other activities he operated a farm and for four years was clerk of the Probate Court of Woodbury, Connecticut, which met in the manse.

His pastorate was marked by the "Great Sickness" of 1727, by frequent religious revivals and by periods of bloody conflict with the Indians. The father of eleven children he lived to the venerable age of 83, 61 of them spent in the ministry — yet, according to one account, he never had a "vacation, a donation party or a nervous prostration."

Three of the next four Stoddards in the direct ancestral line were also clergymen, but Charles, the father of Seneca Ray Stoddard, apparently found a farmer's life more to his liking. He must have been of a rather restless nature because he never seemed to occupy one farm for very long. One of these was near Malone in upstate New York's Franklin County. There he married Julia Ray and there they lived briefly before moving again, this time to a farm in Wilton, town of Moreau, Saratoga County, N.Y.

Charles Stoddard, father of Seneca Ray

This was the birthplace of Seneca Ray. Although May 13 was the month and day of his birth, there seems to be some doubt whether 1843 or 1844 was the correct natal year. In H. P. Smith's monumental *History of Warren Country*, published in 1885, and in the souvenir program published in conjunction with the celebration of the Warren Country Centennial in 1913, the earlier year is cited. However, in the newspaper obituaries and on his tombstone in Pine View Cemetery, Glens Falls, the later year appears.

Both Seneca Ray and his brother Edward were still young when their mother died in 1851. Later on their father married Laura Cook, who bore him three more children — Julia, Frank and Emma — before her death in 1864. Some years afterward, when the children had grown up and were on their own, Charles Stoddard moved once more — this time to Hartford, Michigan, where on January 30, 1874, at the age of 50, he was killed by a falling tree.

Like many other young men of that day, Seneca Ray Stoddard was virtually self taught. Seemingly, he did not show any inclination or liking for farm life because at 19 he left home and went to Green Island, near Troy, where he worked as an ornamental painter in the car works owned by Eaton and Gilbert. The excellent scenes which he painted on the interiors of passenger cars attracted so much favorable attention that within

Miniature composite of Glens Falls views: Hudson River, the village, churches, etc.

six months he took the place of a painter who had received more for a day's work than young Stoddard's weekly wages — three dollars.

In 1864, he moved to Glens Falls, where he followed the business of sign and ornamental painting, but he spent his spare hours doing landscape and portrait work. At the time he was also learning the art of photography because he felt that the camera afforded greater opportunities than did portraiture to record Nature's varying views and moods. As his stock of photographs steadily increased, thereby perpetuating many of the grandest scenes in the nearby mountain and lake region, the prints began to be in considerable demand among tourists and others who heard about their photographic artistry.

In response to this popularity Stoddard gave up shop work and devoted himself entirely to photography.

During this phase of his career it is understandable that most of his photographic subjects were those offered by the great river which flows through Glens Falls. These views, mostly of the Hudson itself and the industries that lined its banks, measured only two by three inches and thereby suffered by contrast with the superb scenes later recorded when he had acquired costlier equipment and more experience. But even those early views, some of them winter scenes, provided convincing proof that Stoddard's compositional skill with paint could be readily translated into similar artistry with the camera.

Shortly afterward, having seemingly exhausted the photographic possibilities near Glens Falls, S. R. began to travel farther afield. By means of the railroad, bicycle, stagecoach, steamboat or livery stable buggy, sometimes even by shank's mare (on foot), he journeyed to such notably picturesque regions as Lakes George and Champlain, Schroon and Luzerne; to the historic ruins of Fort William Henry, Ticonderoga and Fort Frederic, that costly, visible reminder of the French failure at Crown Point.

Gradually the photographer acquired more than local fame. The best evidence of this appeared in the June 1876 issue of the Philadelphia *Photographer* wherein an editor expressed this opinion: "In looking over some of the beautiful views of European scenery, by some of its finest artists, we have often sighed for such work by Americans — and now we have it from Mr. Stoddard. The stereos are perfect gems of photography, but the larger views captivate us most. They seem to be filled with the feeling and expression of the true artist. For choice of subject, arrangement and balance of lines, depth and beauty of perspective, well-chosen and effective foregrounds, clearly-defined yet subdued distances — all these give a charming sense of a real atmosphere which we have never seen excelled."

By that time Stoddard had already made several photographing trips to the Adirondacks and had added the filmed results to his rapidly growing stock. These were sold, along with photographic equipment and sup-

Miniature composite: Hotels of Lake George, Luzerne and Schroon Lake

Miniature composite: Rogers Rock, Ruins of Fort Ticonderoga

23

Miniature composite: "On the Plank," Half Way House, Bloody Pond, Ft. George Hotel

plies, from the small store in his home at 36 Elm Street in Glens Falls. By 1880 his business had grown so well that he issued an illustrated catalog which contained his entire list of more than a thousand selected subjects shown in miniature composite (one-fifth their original diameter) and grouped in clusters of twenty-five each according to the region covered. His views were also being marketed by agents in New York, Boston, Philadelphia, Montreal, London, Paris and Berlin.

Stoddard had now achieved international fame as a camera artist and also demonstrated the first phase of what later became a career of pronounced versatility as a photographer, guidebook writer, mapmaker, artist in oils and other media, author, lecturer, editor, inventor and traveler to distant places not only in America but also in Europe, North Africa and the Near East.

Chapter 2

The Map Series

Although S. R. Stoddard earned early fame as a photographer and guidebook writer, he also became one of the outstanding mapmakers of his time. By nature a very patient and methodical person, he had acquired a sound practical training as a civil engineer while assisting Hiram R. Philo, a well-known Glens Falls surveyor who was the father-in-law of Frank Stoddard, Seneca Ray's brother. It is a matter of record that Philo, besides doing much of the surveying around Lake George, had plotted many of the streets in Glens Falls. This apprenticeship enabled the energetic photographer to add another skill to his impressive array of talents.

The first three annual editions (1874-76) of Stoddard's *Adirondacks Illustrated* contained only three of his maps. The first of these was a detailed pen and ink chart of Ausable Chasm; the second, a rather rough sketch of Schroon Lake; the third, besides showing the few roads and railroads which served the northern region, located the infrequent inns and hotels that accommodated the ever-increasing number of travelers to the alluring Adirondacks.

The next two editions had the same three maps but also featured a somewhat complicated, copyrighted table of distances and travel fares. For its frontispiece the 1879 issue had what the author termed a microscopic map of the wilderness showing the forest resorts and the principal roads leading thereto.

Although all the maps cited were either drawn or adapted by Stoddard, the chart in the cover pocket was not his work but one "prepared by G. W. and C. B. Colton of New York. Even though it was almost identical to Dr. W. W. Ely's superb 1869 map, no credit was given him — on the map itself — by either the publisher or Stoddard. The latter, however, did acknowledge his indebtedness to Ely in the introduction to the 1880 edition of the guidebook.

This issue featured Stoddard's own map of the Adirondacks, a compilation project which occupied considerable time over a period of nearly four years. Stoddard's statement explaining the way that this map was put together is of interest:

"A large portion of the great wilderness has never been surveyed with rod and chain and probably will not be for years to come. To Dr. W. W. Ely, the pioneer in recording these unmapped portions, is due the gratitude of thousands, who have acknowledged the benefit derived from his valuable map which up to the present time has been the only one worthy of the name. With the thousands we sincerely join; in substituting our own in place of his, which has been published annually in connection with this work since its first issue, we do so because the rapid development of certain portions and the growing importance of the whole as a summer resort seem to make a new and more complete work necessary.

"In the construction of the new map all available sources of information have been used. Important points outside the wilderness proper have been determined in accordance with official surveys and connected with the mountains of the interior, whose principal peaks have been accurately located by triangulation (Colvin's surveys). Access has been had to important surveys made under State patronage, and by private parties which are now, for the first time, given to the public in map form. In addition to this reliable material drawings of small sections on an extended scale, covering the entire region, were sent in duplicate for correction by men familiar with the various localities. Thus the map is as complete as possible — careful attention given to proportion and distance; many trails, carries, ponds and streams now appear for the first time on any map.

"Reduced to a uniform scale by photography the result, it is believed, approaches perfection as nearly as can be short of actual trigonometrical survey. It gives altitudes, the location of all hotels and principal camps with roads leading thereto; shows distances in figures on roads, trails and streams and indicates also the nature of the latter in important instances.

"To the gathering, compilation and reduction of the mass of material made use of and its final redrawing from the engraver the entire autumn and winter of 1879 were given."

Besides using such standard earlier maps as those of Asher & Adams, Beers, Benedict, Burr, Gray, Stoddard also was given much information by such local authorities as Dr. G. F. Bixby and H. K. Averill, (civil engineer), both of Plattsburgh and S. J. Farnsworth of Raymondville, whose map of the Raquette River system was considered to be the finest available. Other authorities were T. B. Tate of Ogdensburg, S. D. Andrews of Sageville and A. N. Cheney of Glens Falls. Dr. W. Seward Webb and William W. Durant also provided desired data about their respective extensive holdings around Nehasane and Raquette Lake.

Among the many guides and hotelkeepers consulted were Jesse Corey, Martin Moody, Bill Nye, Ed Otis, J. J. Sevey, Chauncey Smith, Charles Fenton, Tyler Merwin, Fred Bassett, Chauncey Hathorn, Isaac Kenwill, Mitchell Sabattis, John Plumley, Jack Sheppard and Sam Dunakin. Orson (Old Mountain) Phelps, who had previously drawn a somewhat

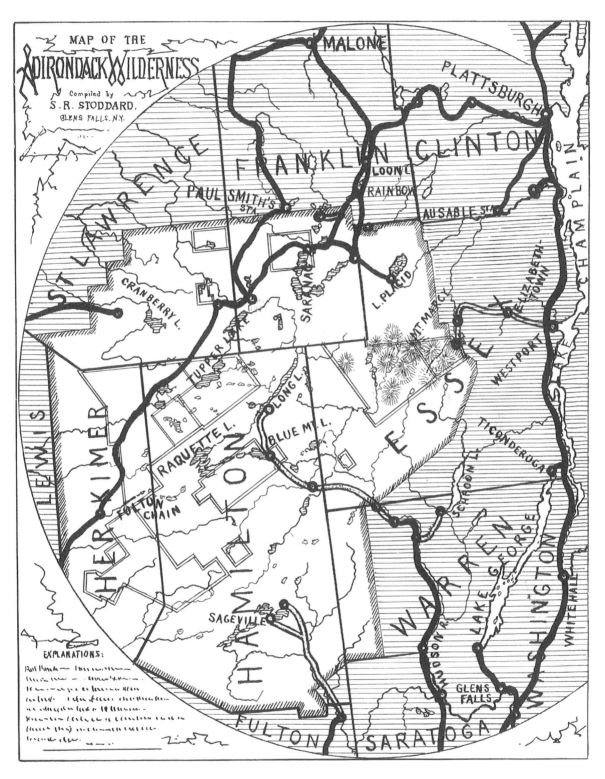

Map of the Adirondacks
Preliminary Sketch

29

crude but nevertheless accurate map of the Keene Valley section, provided many details and names.

The finished map, which was promptly and widely acclaimed as the best of its kind then available, featured an unusual characteristic. Using Mount Marcy as his focal point Stoddard drew a series of concentric circles, the space between each representing an airline distance of ten miles. Thus anyone could readily determine the appropriate distance between that great peak and any other location in the mountains. For the further convenience of the traveler the current railroad, steamboat and stagecoach fares for the various routes were provided as well as distances noted on the roads and trails.

First published in 1881 and continuously incorporating personal notes and the results of government surveys, this map retained the same concentric circle device until only a few years prior to its last issue in 1912. From 1892 on it also indicated the boundaries of the Adirondack Park, established that year with the noteworthy help of Stoddard's illustrated lecture campaign in Albany and throughout the state.

Testimonials to the popularity and reliability of the map included those from the following sources:

Forest and Stream: "An article which is indispensable to the Adirondack tourist is one of Stoddard's new maps of that region. It is the most complete map of that section ever published."

Charles Hallock, author of the *Fishing Tourist:* "I think the map is a marvel of accuracy and detail and complete beyond reasonable expectations."

Fred Mather, author of *My Angling Friends* and assistant to the U. S. Fish Commission: "I have found it most useful in locating the tributaries of streams where I wish to plant fish and I consult it frequently."

A. Judd Northrop, author of *Camps and Tramps in the Adirondacks:* "Stoddard's map seems to be remarkably accurate. The distances given are reliable; indeed the giving of distances so fully is a feature peculiar to this map. The designation of the overflowed lands is also new and valuable."

"Nessmuk" (G. W. Sears), author of *Woodcraft:* "Stoddard's map is the best pocket map I ever carried. I took it on two long canoe cruises and can recall several instances where, when I was a little fogged in the deep woods, the map helped me out. When I lost the first map between Stony Pond and Big Slim, I felt the loss as a real calamity."

Rev. W. H. H. Murray (Adirondack Murray), author of *Adventures in the Wilderness:* "I can cordially commend it to all tourists to the Adirondack region."

Both the New York State Fish and Forestry Commissions bought and used the map extensively in the work of their respective departments. Stoddard's ledgers show that the latter commission alone purchased 1200

MAP OF LAKE CHAMPLAIN.
Section No. 5.

MAP OF LAKE CHAMPLAIN.
Section No. 3.

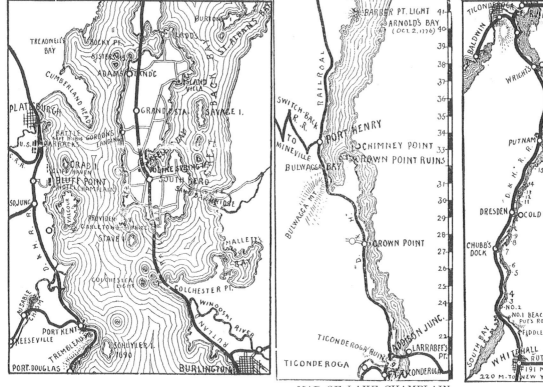

MAP OF LAKE CHAMPLAIN
Section No. 4.

MAP OF LAKE CHAMPLAIN.
Section No. 2.

MAP OF LAKE CHAMPLAIN.
Section No. 1.

Map of Lake Champlain (in sections)

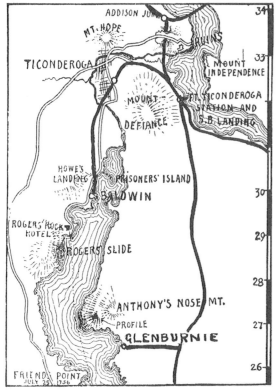

MAP OF LAKE GEORGE.
Section No. 4.

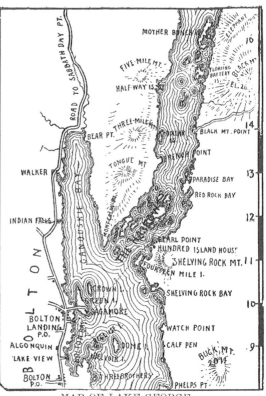

MAP OF LAKE GEORGE.
Section No. 2.

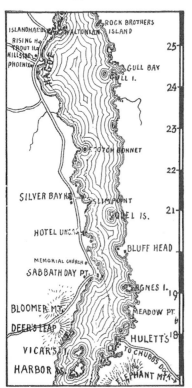

MAP OF LAKE GEORGE.
Section No. 3.

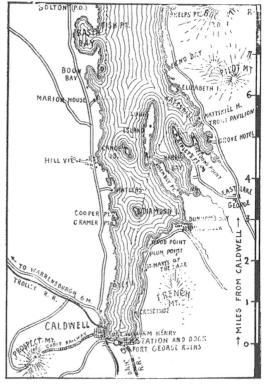

MAP OF LAKE GEORGE.
Section No. 1.

32

Map of Lake George (in sections)

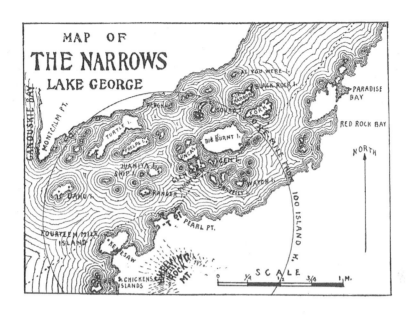

copies. Another sizable order came in 1891 when the Adirondack League Club, undoubtedly the largest sporting club in the world, engaged the Glens Falls mapmaker to publish a chart of their private domain — nearly 200,000 acres or over 275 square miles — in the southern section of the woods.

He also made the official map for the Lake Placid Shoreowners Association in 1901.

Whereas the Adirondack map was a compilation based on official surveys and Stoddard's personal notes, his chart of Lake George represented his own field work in 1880. This four-color project was of particular interest because, besides being an accurate delineation of the lake, it provided the names of all the principal property owners; the location of the numerous hotels; the steamboat routes, roads and railroads. Along both margins of the map were additional features such as detailed plotting of the lakeshore communities — Caldwell, Bolton, Kattskill Bay and Dresden. Approved and adopted by the State Engineer and Surveyor, this map accompanied the report on public lands in 1883. Revised frequently it sold well right up through the final printing in 1915.

In 1890 Stoddard made his first map of Lake Champlain. Like that of the Adirondacks this was also a compilation based partly on government surveys and partly on personal work and notes. On a scale of 2½ miles to an inch the great lake of the Iroquois was shown in elaborate detail. Besides tinted marginal maps of Lake George, the lake from Whitehall to Ticonderoga and the course of the Richelieu River, distances were also cited from Burlington, Plattsburgh, Port Kent and Westport to other areas of interest and to eastern seaboard cities. This map, very much in demand, went through eleven revisions before 1911, the last year of its publication.

Unquestionably the major mapmaking effort made by S. R. Stoddard was his hydrographic chart of Lake George. This survey occupied most of his time and attention during the period from 1906 to 1908. The difficulty and time-consuming nature of such an assignment can be best understood when one recalls that this lovely lake, The American Como, is thirty-six miles long and from one to three miles wide. Assisted by R. J. Brown, civil engineer of Bolton, Stoddard plotted the topography of the lake and its numerous islands. With the help of Charles Oblenis, his brother-in-law, and occasionally that of George Slade, city engineer of Glens Falls, the many thousands of soundings were painstakingly recorded. The deep soundings were done by Capt. Lee Harris of East Lake George, Alex Taylor of Bolton, Gillette Bartlett of Sabbath Day Point and George Cook of Baldwin. Capt. Wesley Finkle and Walter Harris charted the steamship courses.

This five-foot chart, drawn on a scale of three miles to an inch, was copyrighted each year to cover the various sections as they were completed. The entire map was copyrighted in 1910 and was reprinted in 1951. All through the intervening years it has been a boon to boatmen and fishermen, not only for its locating the various navigational hazards, but also for the inclusion of twelve helpful panoramic views of the principal landmarks and shoreline features.

In 1908 Stoddard started still another enterprise. From that year until 1915 the industrious man from Glens Falls made two trips annually to gather information about hotels and road conditions for a new type of map. Entitled *Picturesque Trips Through the Adirondacks in an Automobile*, this project divided the region into fourteen sections and contained many accompanying ads and illustrations. Most of the latter were of the newer hotels but there were also photos of the older resorts which had advertised in the very earliest editions of *The Adirondacks Illustrated*. Of special interest were the enlargements and improvements which prosperity had made possible for the owners of such places down through the heyday years.

About 15,000 of these auto-road-maps, as Stoddard called them, were sold each year. Since very few of the roads, particularly those in sparsely settled sections of the Adirondacks, were anything but adequate during the infancy of the automobile, Stoddard, the traveler, understandably became an ardent, persistent and effective advocate of good highways.

So, by his maps of the Adirondacks, Lake George and Lake Champlain and finally his road maps, Stoddard gave still another proof of his remarkable industry and versatility.

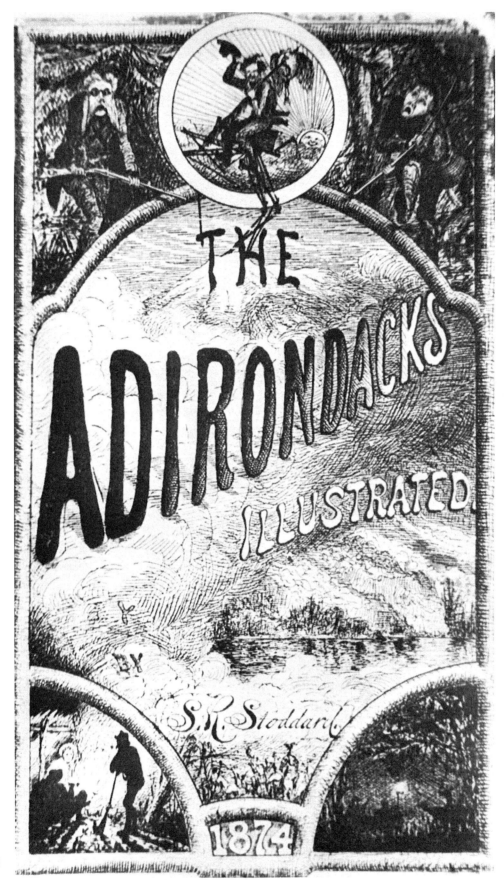

36

Chapter 3

The Guidebook Series

Wherever Stoddard went on his photographic trips, he was also busily occupied in collecting the information and making the observations he needed for his later projects — his guidebooks and his maps. By early 1871 he had assembled the views he wanted for his first venture, a modest little booklet which he entitled *Lake George*. In the brief preface he explained that this effort was not intended to be a guidebook or a complete history of the lake but only a book of pictures telling of things most noted and answering questions most often asked.

There were only eleven views in all: Lake George from the south; the Fort William Henry Hotel; the ruins of old Fort William Henry; Tea, Recluse and Sloop Islands; views of Bolton, the Narrows, Black Mountain, Sabbath Day Point and, for good measure, the ruins at Fort Ticonderoga.

Encouraged by the success of this first publication venture, the photographer had ready for the next season a much more ambitious work with the same title. This small volume, besides containing etchings by Stoddard, also had woodcuts by the Sears, Chubb and Ferguson Company. Both types of illustrations were made by John McGuire of Albany, who, instead of using the ordinary method of "cutting" with acid, had "built up" by galvanic action. The results, while showing the imperfections of newness, were a decided improvement over the illustrations in the previous booklet.

In the preface the author showed samples of his clever way with words which made this and his long succession of guidebooks so readable and so popular. "Although my main object is to give information (for a consideration), I may occasionally slop over into sentiment, but will try not to afflict my readers very often in that way. While for the benefit of such as are in constant danger of making such mistakes, I will point out places where it is considered eminently proper to go into ecstasies over scenery, etc.

"I am not going to write a history, however, because the wear and tear on the ordinary brain must be immense; moreover, the country is full of histories. All others who have written of the silvery lake have made discoveries. I have not. I regret exceedingly that such is the case. I have, however, served the principal events up in a new dress and, in the light of later revelations, twisted some of the old ones about so as to answer every purpose. But, since it all happened sometime ago, it is consequently of little interest to the general reader and has therefore been given in small doses which may be skipped at pleasure for the hotels and other things of the present day."

After crediting Dr. A. W. Holden and other friends for their assistance, Stoddard continued engagingly: "Prefaces are detestable and seldom read, but if nothing was created in vain the writer hopes that by putting this excuse among the legitimate reading matter some absent-minded ones may possibly struggle through to the end before discovering their mistakes. Thus they will become acquainted with a few of the reasons and perhaps think kindly of him who now bids farewell to earthly fears and wades shiveringly into the surging sea of literature."

During that same year (1873) Stoddard also published *Ticonderoga: Past and Present*. This thin book was apparently not so successful as the other guidebooks because it was not put out again.

The next season the energetic author decided to increase his coverage because there followed a series of four annually revised books called *Lake George, Saratoga, Luzerne and Schroon Lake*. Then for the next three years (1878-1880) Stoddard resumed the original Lake George title but started including more and more Saratoga material while deleting matter about Luzerne and Schroon Lake.

The issues for 1881-1888 still retained the featuring of Lake George but Saratoga now shared the title. In these two editions Stoddard employed a novel type of format. The Saratoga section was stamped as such on the back of the cover but its contents were printed upside down so that its text would not be confused with the other portion relating to Lake George. From 1889 until 1915, the forty-first and final year of the publication of this useful and much-used series, the title changed to include Lake Champlain. Some of the editions had maps, others did not but the separate map especially compiled for these regions made up for the omission.

During this same period (1874-1914) Stoddard also issued another guidebook, *The Adirondacks Illustrated*. During that forty-year span these little books became the most popular and widely-used items of their kind. They included maps, routes for canoe, rail, stage and walking trips and provided much historical and descriptive information. Although very readable it is true that this series usually proved to be somewhat disappointing to historians in search of facts. Some of the editions lacked complete information about the hotels, their owners' names, the rates and capacities.

E. R. Wallace's *Guide to the Adirondacks* (1875-1899) contained more of such factual material but never did gain the wide popularity of Stoddard's product. The latter was a wittier writer as well as an artist and photographer. Therefore his illustrations were more original, authentic and effective than most of those found in the other series.

Another reason for the greater popularity of the Stoddard books can be attributed to the entertaining narrative which he later called *Old Times in the Adirondacks.* This series, which started with the first issue of the guidebook, served as the narrative thread on which was strung the changes of succeeding years. It was dropped by the author in 1893 with the following explanation:

"Changes? Wild grass grows on the old routes and the unknown places of then are now centers of a summer population greater than the total of all Adirondack visitors of twenty years ago (1873).

"Railroads now encircle the Adirondacks like the iron frame of a landing net. From the encircling lines others penetrate the interior, crossing each other and branching in turn to reach important points, or lose themselves among the mountains or in the watery highways that are woven in a network all over the lake region of the west.

"So the old Narrative *(Old Times in the Adirondacks)* is dropped and the space given to that which is believed to be of more general value to the tourist, condensed and in a more convenient size for the pocket."

This story of the author's first long trip through the Adirondacks in 1873 prompted the editor of the Plattsburgh *Republican* to make the following discerning statement: "Mr. Stoddard is better and better known year by year as a humorous writer of marked ability. His works which have already been published exhibit qualities which will yet entitle him to no mean place in the galaxy of funny fellows."

Other representative testimonials include the following:

The Albany *Evening Journal:* "Routes, fares, timetables, maps and whatever else the traveler is most interested in knowing are treated clearly and intelligently."

Thomas Cook & Son: "Stoddard's are the most valuable guidebooks to these districts. We are able to dispose of a large number of them annually to tourists. We know of no better or more convenient books published for these resort areas."

Brentano Brothers, New York: "Your *Adirondack Guide* has a largely increasing sales in our stores with each year. Its excellent arrangement and annual revision makes it practically the only guide to that region that can be relied upon as being entirely trustworthy and up to date."

The New York *Times:* "It is a book that can be read from beginning to end at any time and be found full of interesting reading matter."

The Troy *Times:* "It is a delightful book, well spiced with anecdote and adventure and will serve either for pleasant reading at home or as a reliable guide to the traveler in the regions described."

Baker & Taylor, New York: "For several years past we have, as wholesale booksellers, sold your Guides to the Adirondacks and Lake

George. We have found the sales larger each year and far in excess of the combined sales of all other similar books. The accuracy of your maps as well as the reliability of your descriptions we have personally checked and in our experience rely implicitly upon them."

Such complimentary remarks bear out the conviction that S. R. Stoddard was gaining wide recognition as a successful guidebook writer as well as an eminent photographer.

Chapter 4

Through the Adirondacks in 1873

By the late 1860's S. R. Stoddard had already taken many photographs of the scenic spots in the Glens Falls-Saratoga-Luzerne-Lake George-Ticonderoga region. Since this was the era of the stereopticon, most of the views were made double for use in the still-fascinating device. But the enterprising camera artist also marketed smaller versions of most of the same subjects.

Stoddard used whatever means of transportation that was available to reach the desired points of photographic interest. By stagecoach, steamboat, guideboat, buckboard, bicycle, railroad and often as not on shank's mare (on foot) the incredibly industrious cameraman gradually extended the scope of his picture-taking activities.

Moreover, he was also taking full advantage of the opportunity to gather factual and historical material supplemented by personal observation which he later used in his guidebook and map series.

The first trip beyond his usual photographic periphery was made in 1870 by Stoddard and Charles Oblenis, his brother-in-law and assistant (the Professor of the series). On that journey the two men visited Ausable Chasm, photographed it as thoroughly as possible in the light of the inaccessibility of many of its scenic features at that time, then went on for a brief vacation in the Adirondacks. No details are available giving their exact itinerary on that journey, although it is known that they were in the Blue Mountain-Long Lake region for several days.

The second excursion was recorded graphically and amusingly in the thirteen-chapter series which Stoddard printed in his *Adirondacks Illustrated* and again in his *Northern Monthly*, a short-lived, eminently readable but financially unsuccessful magazine venture. This journal covers the twenty-two day trek which started at Glens Falls on Sept. 26, 1873 and terminated at the same place on Oct. 18th of that year.

The travelers entered the mountains from the east by way of Lake Champlain. Since the railroad which follows the west shore of the Lake had not yet been completed, the iron horse took them only as far as Whitehall, where they boarded the Vermont II, the largest of the Champlain steamers, for the meandering voyage northward to Port Kent.

Stoddard described his brother-in-law and himself in the following facetious manner: "The Professor is not actually a professor nor is he stupendous either in length, breadth or thickness and not particular about his diet; perish the thought! He simply abstains from the absorption of that mysterious compound known as hash on account of the uncertainty of its origin. He revolts at the sight of sausages as they are unpleasantly suggestive of a dear little dog he once owned and loved. Can't endure cream in his coffee because it 'looks so, floating round on top!' and whose heart bleeds and appetite vanishes if an unlucky fly chances to take a hot bath in his tea. To these peculiarities add a disposition to see the fun in his own forlornness and with boyishness dyed in the wool and the Professor stands before you.

"As for Stoddard himself suffice it to say that nature was very lavish in the bestowal of longitude, although not noticeably so in regard to latitude. He was given also a disposition to dare and a physical development capable of enduring a vast amount of arduous rest. Thus you have the dainty Professor and the ease-loving photographer and enthusiastic sportsman. Neither of us carried a gun, rod, umbrella or other instrument of death but were armed only with cameras, sketchpads, notebooks and hearts to drink in the glories of the great wild woods. We were bound for the mountains to get health and strength for frames not over-strong."

Rockwell, the chief pilot of the famous vessel and a rapid-fire conversationalist, was depicted mixing sociability and sailing orders . . . "Steady now! . . . Good evening, gentlemen. I know your voice — up a little! — Steady! — let me see — let her run — oh yes I remember now. I saw you — hold her there! — last summer, you came up here and this other gentleman was with you. I didn't recognize your voice at first — hard over! That light's out again — you are a little hoarse, ought to take something for that.

"Crowd her against the bank there, let her chaw, the reachon will clear her! — wished he could — luff a point, boys! — pass his life among the grand old mountains — hug the shore a little closer! — and look through nature up to nature — wind a little flawy and she's down at the head."

Then he sandwiched Beecher between Susan B. Anthony and Victoria C. Woodhull, said she was light aft and clawed to starboard; asked if we could fully endorse Prof. Tyndall's theory of nebular hegira. He ruined the reputation of Andromeda and Cassiopoeia and other heavenly bodies by hopelessly entangling them with Butler and Massachusetts politics . . . He thought the Greek slave a perfect figure, said she sucked mud through here sometimes and they had to be careful of her flues. Admired Joan of Arc — said she carried an awful head of steam but her boilers were undoubtedly good or else Mr. Root would have made a fuss over them.

Then he remarked that Phil Sheridan was a brick, "Just as full of fun as an egg of meat." The General himself had told him a story which happened one day at the Thousand Islands. Sheridan, who had wandered off alone, came across an old farmer with whom he entered into conversation and ended by offering him a drink from his brandy flask. The old fellow took a generous swig and, when pressed, even an encore. Then, as the General was leaving, the farmer suddenly called, 'Who be ye that I've had the honor of drinkin' with?'

'My name's Sheridan,' replied the famous fighter.

'No, be it now? Ye ain't any relation to Gineral Sheridan, be ye?'

'Well, rather. You see I am General Sheridan.'

'Ye ain't though,' said the old farmer who had a profound respect for the hero of Winchester, whom he considered the greatest man living! 'Hev I bin drinkin' with the Gineral himself?'

'Yes, sir,' said little Phil, pompously straightening up and enjoying the effects of his words, 'you have had the honor of a drink out of General Philip Sheridan's own flask!'

The old chap gazed at the short, thick-set form before him for a moment; then a "sold" expression crept over his face. Finally, when his look of blended wonder and reverence had changed to disgust, he growled out, 'Not-by-a-dam-sight-little-feller. Gineral-Sheridan's- over-seven-feet-tall!'

The "Vermont" docked at Port Kent early the next morning. There the passengers got into the waiting stagecoaches and set out for Keeseville over the jolting of a plank road which seemed more like corduroy. A rough three-mile trip brought the brothers-in-law to the Chasm House at Ausable Chasm. This hotel, a made-over, spacious private residence, had accommodations for about twenty guests and was run at the time by H. H. Bromley, a jolly, easy-going sort of fellow, with an ecstatic, staccato laugh.

The next morning Stoddard and Oblenis visited the miniature Yosemite, only parts of which had previously been safe to visit. Earlier that same year (1873), however, a company of Philadelphians had bought nearly all the surrounding land, had started the construction of a hotel nearby and built stairways, galleries and bridges so that nearly the entire length could now be traversed with comfort; the remainder in a boat.

From Ausable Chasm they went to wide-awake Keeseville, made prosperous by its immense waterpower resources which were utilized by twine, wire and horseshoe nail manufacturers. Then past Clintonville with its said-to-be largest forge on the continent and its decayed, ashy, sooty look, to Ausable Forks. There they proceeded part way on foot to Wilmington, which had a deserted, worn-out look in late September. Two or three shut-up looking stores, three shut-up looking churches, an old forge; saw, starch and grist mills. The place was owned long before by a Major Sanford, who came there, built two or three stills and went to making whiskey. "Those were the times when it wasn't a sin to make it," said Stoddard's informant. "Well, he went to making whiskey, built mills

Whiteface Mtn.—Three Braves. L to R: Williams, owner of Whiteface Mtn. House, Charles Oblenis, brother-in-law of Seneca Ray Stoddard, S. R. Stoddard

and that brick church over there and then failed. Next George Weston came here with $10,000, cut a road to the top of the mountain (Whiteface) and built a little house up there. But he soon lost all his money and sold out to Sidney Weston of Winooski, Vermont, who is smart as lightning and will make it pay if any living man can."

The next day Baldwin, their warm-hearted landlord, reluctantly agreed to accompany them on the ascent of Whiteface. Two miles from the hotel they left the wagon and proceeded up the rocky bridle path toward the summit. Great rocks alternated with pools of black muck to make the trail so treacherous that the two visitors wondered how humanity-loaded horses could ever negotiate such a precarious path.

After a brief lunch stop at the cozy shanty in the clearing three-fourths of a mile from the top, they added their names to those displayed in every reachable place in the building and then clambered the rest of the way up to the peak.

"Pretty rough work," said Baldwin, the guide, "but hundreds of people come up here every year and ride clear to the top. A big doctor from Buffalo once came up here with his family and a very valuable four-horse team that he had been all over the country with. When he said that he was going to the top of the mountain, I tried to stop him and offered, for nothing, to get him some horses that were accustomed to the road rather than have him hurt his. But no; 'Other horses have been there, haven't they?' he asked, and when I said yes he answered, 'then mine can get up there, too!'

"So he took them out of the harness and put his wife, a woman that would go about 200, on the fieriest one of the lot and started. I felt bad because I knew something would happen.

"Well, sir, they rode those horses to the very top and then just turned around and - - -." The guided men gazed down over the fearful precipice at their feet and their hearts seemed to cease their beating as he slowly concluded - - - "and rode them right back down again!"

"But how can ladies manage to keep on the horses' backs where it seems almost impossible for the animal to get along alone?" I asked.

"Manage!" said he, "like a man of course! It makes me laugh to see them sometimes when they find out that they've got to ride that way. So modest when they start — some of them. They are dreadfully ashamed of even showing their feet at first, but they soon get over that and come down with colors flying, I tell you!

"I don't know as they would ever have done it if Mrs. Murray, wife of the Rev. Adirondack Murray, hadn't set the fashion. She's a dashing, independent sort of a woman who doesn't let thoughts of what people might say interfere with her plans. Well! after Mrs. Murray set the example, we had no difficulty. Now lots of them go up that way. With the horses we have and a guide at their side, there is not the slightest danger."

On the topmost point, firmly attached to the rock, they found the card of the chief of the Adirondack Survey, a copper disc with this inscription: Whiteface Mountain Station No. 2 Verplanck Colvin, S.N.Y. Adirondack Survey, 1872. The surface of the surrounding rock was already scarred and chiseled with names of former visitors. Nearby, as if to rebuke the frivolity of such little thoughts and minds, stretching far across the level and cut deep and clear were the words: "Thanks be to God for the Mountains!"

On the descent Baldwin took the lead and made a desperate effort to keep his feet from getting the advantage of him. His ax, tin pail and sundry other articles jingled and thumped against his sides. Finally he stopped and exclaimed, "It bothers me to have folks treading on my heels. You'd better take the lead." And so they did.

Later that night Baldwin was overheard to say that it certainly beat somethun-or-other how them fellows came down that mountain. "And when I'd get some ways behind and drop into a little dogtrot to catch up, I'd hear that little fellow (Oblenis) snicker. Then away they'd go hell-a-ty-split and I do believe that that long-legged one (Stoddard) would cover six feet at every step!"

The next day the two men from Glens Falls hired a carriage and driver and headed for North Elba through the Wilmington Notch, which Stoddard considered to be one of the finest — if not the finest — combination of river, rock and mountain scenery to be found in the Adirondacks. It was especially beautiful as they saw it in its autumn dress that early October day. Although their enjoyment of the day was somewhat marred by the breakdown of the rented carriage, they were able to continue their trip aboard a buckboard which providentially appeared.

Drawn by two ancient specimens of horse architecture whose backs were crossed and covered by straps until they looked like a railroad map of Massachusetts, the conveyance was nevertheless sturdy. The colored driver was also headed for North Elba, the home and burial place of the bones of John Brown, the Old Man of Ossawatomie. Since only fourteen years had elapsed since he (Brown), three sons and eighteen others had fought and died for the Negroes at Harper's Ferry, Stoddard fully expected that this young man would know a great deal about the fanatical benefactor of his race. But he proved to be a disappointingly poor source of information as well as the last of his kind in North Elba. The others, some fifteen or twenty families had long since departed.

"What has become of them?" asked the photographer.

" 'Don't know, they couldn't make a livin' heah. Too cold for 'em. Wan't much used to work, I guess, an' couldn't stan' the kind they got heah. Most of 'em was barbers an' sich who thought they wouldn't have nothin' to do when they came heah. So, after the Old Man (Brown) died, they couldn't get along noway. And they dug out some of 'em an' some of 'em died. An' Gur-r-r, one old fellah froze to death!' "

Soon afterward Stoddard and Oblenis resumed their journey with Att. Clyne, who had improvised a whiffletree to replace the broken one. A short time later they came to a place where the houses were a little nearer together than anywhere else along the road, so they called it North Elba. In 1873, as now, the population was rather thin and the country was to a great extent devoted to grazing and grass growing. Winter seemed to be the chief season and it never disappointed them in coming. Then, as now, it was seldom that a year passed when snow was not seen on the nearby mountains in every month but August.

According to jokester Att. Clyne, their Ausable Forks driver, North Elba was said to be very healthy, so much so that the only manner of taking off was a habit the inhabitants had of freezing to death. When this happened, as was often the case in summer, they never found it necessary to bury them. They simply laid them away somewhere exposed to the pure balsamic air and in the course of six or seven weeks they mossed over. Clyne facetiously added that John Brown was only covered up as a protection against curiosity hunters, who have a habit of chopping off pieces of fossils and the like and who have broken off pieces of his tombstone to the extent that it had to be boxed up to keep enough for directory purposes.

They found the grave strewn with faded flowers; a florist's leaden cross and crown filled with a sodden mass lay on the little mound and under it the bones of Old John Brown — alone. Of his large family not one remained to watch over him, but in their place, strangers, who knew less about him than they (Stoddard and Oblenis), who lived far away. His widow and five of his twenty children were still living, scattered over the West, some of them in California.

In spite of the persistent efforts made by the people who had converted the old Abolitionist's farmhouse into an inn, the travelers went on to the North Elba Hotel. This hostelry, two miles from Lake Placid, was then owned by a Mr. Lyon, a man of many talents. Besides being the postmaster and justice of the peace, he took a fatherly interest in everything going on in the tiny community.

The next day found the two men in Lake Placid, which then had only two hotels — Nash's near the north end of Mirror Lake and nearby the Lake Placid House, usually spoken of as Brewster's. J. V. Nash, proprietor of the former hotel, and well known and liked by sportsmen, was one of the oldest settlers in the immediate neighborhood.

After dinner they succeeded in removing Clyne, their driver, from the presence of a fascinating divinity in calico and started for Saranac Lake. Then, as they neared that place, they decided to push on to Paul Smith's by way of Bloomingdale. This place had a very pretty name, a very new-looking hotel, a very few houses, a very good-looking frame which was started for a church but which then stood considerably darkened by time, patiently waiting to be roofed and clapboarded.

Edmond's Ponds, North Elba, Lake Placid

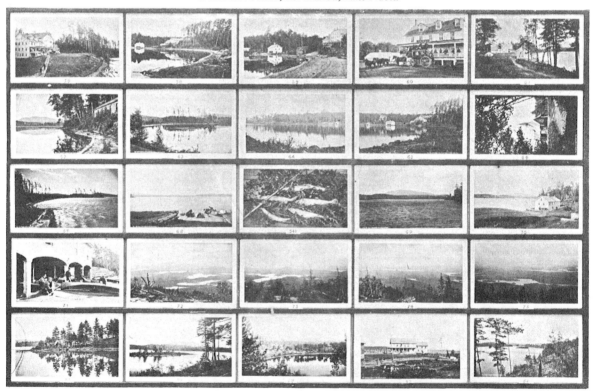

Paul Smith's, St. Regis, and Rainbow Lakes

From there on in to Paul Smith's the trip became very unpleasant. The driver, who didn't know the way but claimed he did, cost them valuable time in the race against an impending storm which soon came down on their umbrellaless heads, trickled down their necks and settled in the seat beneath them.

Att., the driver, was comical and full of spirits. He gave every guidepost a critical examination. At one crossroad, in the darkness he got out, hugged, kicked and grunted up to the shingle on the top of the post. Then after sacrificing sundry matches, with his eyes and fingers and great difficulty, succeeded in finding out that he could not tell anything about it. Thereupon he slid down and in a drizzly, uncertain sort of way got back into the carriage again.

"This road isn't much traveled," opined Att.

"Never mind, don't you see the telegraph?" Shortly afterward the wagon gave a lurch to one side and nearly lost its load; then it brought up and went the other way. Finally, after jerking about like a man with two wooden legs trying to get down a flight of stairs, the buggy came to rest at the bottom of a gully which had been dug out by some freshet and considered so bad that they had built a road around it rather than repair it.

A little farther on they saw a dusky strip of water through a grove of tall pines and on the shore a large house, from which lights gleamed and welcomed them onward. Soon they were seated around a crackling fire in a room full of guides, dogs and sportsmen who smoked and told stories until midnight. Then the two withdrew and went to sleep listening to the patter of the rain on the roof.

Paul Smith's was a surprise to them as it had been to everyone else — an astonishing mixture of fish and fashion, pianos and puppies, Brussels carpeting and cowhide boots. Surrounded by dense forest, out of the way of all travel save its own, near the best hunting and fishing grounds, it was a first-class watering place set right in the midst of the howling wilderness. "Around the house the timid deer roam; within, they rest. Without, the noble buck crashes through the tangled forest; within, he straddles elegantly over the billiard tables and talks horse. On the lake theoretical veterans cast all manner of flies; in the parlors the contents of huge Saratoga trunks are scientifically played and nets are spread for a different kind of fish. Poodles and pointers, hounds, setters, dandies and others of the species are found. Feathers and fishing rods, point lace and pint bottles are variously mixed. Embryo Nimrods — who never knew a more destructive weapon than a yardstick — are seen hung all around with revolvers and game-bags and cartridge-pouches and sporting guns that are fearfully and wonderfully made. Here, you must know, danger is to be faced. Even the ladies bare arms, and at such times are very dangerous sportsmen indeed.

"In appearance Paul (Apollos A.) is not a man you would pick out as the one to keep a popular hotel. He is rather above medium height, usually quiet, not appearing to have much to say about the house nor much to do but listen to and tell stories and perform other like laborious duties usually expected of a keeper of a summer hotel. But somebody there — Mrs. Smith undoubtedly — possesses executive ability, for all seems to go as smoothly as clockwork.

"Although it was rather late in the season when we were there, a few kindred spirits still lingered; these were personally and intimately acquainted with everybody from the Shah and Yankee Sullivan down to the Heathen Chinee and who, when night came, would gather around the stove in the office. There, to the accompaniment of dogs, guides and themselves, review the drama, the arts and sciences, tell stories of fighting men and ministers, dogs and horses, hunting and fishing, interspersed with intensely interesting debates on the relative merits of plug and fine-cut tobacco, and learned disquisitions on the proper position of the left auricle at that exciting moment when the fly had been cast and a gamey two-ounce trout has struck and hesitates as to the expediency of taking to the woods or the open fields.

"On this much-vexed question authorities differ, and it is probable that it will always be a disputed point, as the physical development and temperament of the fish has to be taken into consideration. A fisherman that is a fisherman must be governed by circumstances — in fact must be a strategist of superior caliber, even like unto that of the most successful fisherman of whom we have any record who, after the fashion in those primitive days before they used flies as extensively as at present, swallowed a whale and after a three days' struggle brought him to land."

The next morning, October 7th, finding that the ground was white with snow, they took a stage to Martin's, 14 miles away at the north end of Lower Saranac Lake. "It was a good road too — for a dyspeptic or one troubled with a poor appetite." The driver was apparently in a hurry. Although the ride cost them six dollars, they got their money's worth. "It was a good stage, too. Since we were the only occupants, we had a choice of positions — and tried several. We braced ourselves in the corners, we rattled around, we shot from side to side, and made some good runs, caromed on each other and pocketed ourselves under the seats. We couldn't get knocked out for the sides — excepting a lock-out hole — were buttoned down and the roof was firm — we were satisfied of that for we tried it. Sometimes the Professor's side would rise up to get over a big stone and he would start for me. I had striven with him repeatedly and remonstrated against such frequent and energetic calls and unceremonious visitations — but to no effect. Retribution was sure to follow, however, for when his side went down I would sail majestically over and light on him.

"That vehicle meandered playfully over stones and stumps and into holes. It would hump over logs when we, rising like young eagles, would soar away toward the roof. We liked to soar, but to alight was the question. It would go down into deep holes and stop in such a decided way that we

Saranac Lake, Martin's, Bartlett's, Prospect House

Long Lake, Elizabethtown, Keene Valley

51

would involuntarily feel our heads, expecting to find our backbones sticking up through our hats. When at long last we reached Saranac Lake, it was with a feeling of 'goneness' peculiar to those who have been without food for days and days."

William F. Martin, the innkeeper, came there in 1849 and built a small house for the accommodation of sportsmen. He was among the very first in the wilderness to attempt a sporting house. Accommodating about 200 guests, his place was quite popular although not as fashionable as Paul Smith's in the society sense of the word.

On the following morning Stoddard and the Professor were rowed through Lower Saranac and Round Lakes to Bartlett's Carry and then walked the short distance to the Hotel. This was a long, low, old-fashioned structure built to accommodate about 50 guests. The interior was pleasant, containing some well-furnished rooms, and the food was excellent. Virgil Bartlett, the owner, was a short, thick-set man with a brusque way of speaking that sounded cross until one caught the kindly twinkle in his eyes. He had just made up his mind to give up the business.

"Yes," said he, "I've had enough of it. I've slaved as long as I'm going to and I'm going to sell out. Never'll take another boarder as long as I live — unless it's some old friend like Dr. Ely, for instance."

On October 9th, the fourteenth day of the trip, the brothers-in-law arrived at Kellogg's Hotel in Long Lake, having followed the water route through the Raquette River. Besides the exceptional scenery the principal attraction there was Mitchell Sabattis, the noted Indian guide. Earnest, intelligent and thrifty, a truly devoted member of the Methodist Church, he was also an authority on Indian history. Moreover, he had probably seen more of wood-life than any other man in the wilderness. A fearless and successful hunter he was considered by other guides to have the best knowledge of the woods of them all.

Stoddard attended church that Sunday and heard an earnest discourse from a minister who was also blacksmith, lawyer, shoemaker and merchant in a small way besides devoting his leisure hours to meditation and farming. Over the pulpit was an immense marine clock, great in display of gold, while letters on its face explained that it was presented by Dr. Todd's Mission Sunday School. The photographer remarked on the vast difference between the rendition of familiar pieces by that choir and the high-spiced variety of sacred song sung by the $20,000 kind.

The visitors also watched a Long Lake guideboat being built. The regulation boat, 14 to 17 feet long, and 3 feet wide, weighed from 60 to 80 pounds and cost about a dollar per pound. It was considered to be the synonym for all that was graceful and perfect in that line.

A half-mile carry after a short boatride brought them to Buttermilk Falls — Murray's "Phantom Falls." Here the water dashes and foams down over the rocks, making a descent of about 25 feet; the name though not very poetical, was probably suggested by the churning it gets in reaching

52

Buttermilk Falls, Raquette River

Forked Lake, Tupper Lake, Bog River, Falls

53

the bottom.

"Murray's talk about shooting the falls in his boat in pursuit of the phantom form is a very probable story for a minister to tell," said Blanchard, their guide, with a contemptuous shrug. "It would sound better from one of us guides though. Why I drove a brood of ducks down over there once. The old one knew better than to go — she flew upstream — but they — a dozen of the young ones — went over and only three came out alive. *He* talked of doing it! There isn't Baptist enough about him, but there's one thing he *can* shoot: that's a long bow."

Stoddard's comment on that outburst: "Alas for Mr. Murray's reputation for veracity. The beautiful pictures conjured up by his fertile brain are held as witnesses against him. And that simply because he, in his lavish generosity enriched the common occurrences of everyday life in the woods with the precious increase of conceptive genius, leaving a dazzled world to separate the real from the ideal! The guides take him literally and have come to the conclusion generally that if his preaching is not a better guide to heaven than his book on the Adirondacks, his congregation might manage to worry along with a cheaper man."

On Osprey Island, more popularly known as Murray's Island, they found the bark shanty of old Alvah Dunning. Two or three dogs came out with their master to meet them — not exactly welcome them because the dogs and he growled; therefore the suddenly-conceived idea of spending the night there was just as quickly banished by his surly permission.

"Old Alvah was in his normal condition — suffering from ill treatment. He has *always* been a sufferer because he doesn't always look at things in the same light as others. He believes to this day that it was only by chance, aided somewhat by an overruling Providence, that his life is spared; for did not Ned Buntline, the terrible, chase him all over Blue Mountain Lake with intent to deposit lead in his venerable cuticle? It is said that he hunted for Ned one summer and a misunderstanding arose, to settle which Alvah felt called upon to embezzle a boat of the novelist's and, after perforating it in various places, to sink it in the lake. This manner of procedure struck Ned as being out of order, so as a preliminary move he shot the old man's dog one day while the animal was standing between his master's legs. Alvah was grieved thereby, and with a longing to indulge in cremation, threatened to set fire to the Eagle's Nest.

"When asked about the affair, Ned said, 'I drove him out of that section because he threatened my life. The Old Rip steered clear of me after he found that I was as ready to throw lead as he was threats!'"

The next day the travelers passed the Eagle's Nest, once the wilderness home of Ned Buntline, now a comfortable stopping place for tourists in the summer months. "This strange man with the blended nature of the tiger and the lark, the tender imaginings of a young girl and the uncontrolled passions of a wild beast, came there in 1856 that he might escape the dangers of civilization. Here he had his alternate fierce battles and lov-

54

ing make-ups with his greatest enemy — the bottle. He gave the place and the lakes around the names they now bear; he lived there at odd times until the war cloud broke over the South, when his restless, venturesome nature called him to the field. Out of the war he came unscathed, but the end is not yet — whether it will be up through clearer paths to light, or downward with his life-long foe, cannot be foretold."

Alvah Dunning's camp on Raquette Lake. Dunning on extreme left

Ned Buntline (Edward Z. G. Judson). Sarony photograph.

Chapter 5

Through the Adirondacks in 1873

The following day they passed the shanty owned by the famed artist, A. F. Tait, on South Pond. After a half-mile carry, they were rowed the rest of the way up Long Lake to Kellogg's, where they astonished the proprietor by the earnest manner in which they devoted themselves to business at the dinner table.

After dinner they chartered a seat in a farmer's wagon and went to "Aunt Polly's" at Newcomb and spent the Sabbath with its genial owner, John Davis.

On Monday morning, with knapsacks on their backs, they started for Adirondac, the ruined village among the mountains, 18 miles distant. At Tahawus, locally called the Lower Works, the two stopped at the home of John Cheney, the mighty hunter, partly to see him and partly because they were hungry and wanted dinner. They were disappointed in the first respect — the old man had gone hunting with some of the boys, but not in the second desire because the meal was enjoyable. Mrs. Cheney, a pleasant, cheery, chatty person talked about her absent husband. "Even if he is 73 years old," she remarked, "he can run in the woods now and beat most any of 'em when he feels like it. If you could see him and he happens to feel all right, you could find out a good deal about him. But he's awful changeable — either awful good or awful bad."

After Stoddard had returned to Glens Falls, Cheney wrote him a lengthy letter in which he recounted many of his hunting experiences and close brushes with death.

A ten-mile walk brought the photographer and his companion to the Upper Works and the deserted village of Adirondac. At the head of the street was the old furnace, a part of one chimney still standing; another, shattered by a lightning bolt, lay in ruins at its feet. The water wheel, emblem of departed power, lay motionless save as piece by piece it fell away. Huge blocks of iron, piles of rusty ore, charcoal bursting from the crumbling kilns, great shafts broken and bent, rotting timbers, stones and rubbish lay in one common grave over which loving nature had thrown a shroud of creeping vine.

Near the center of the village was a large house, said at one time to have accommodated a hundred boarders but now grim and silent. Moore, the caretaker, and his wife welcomed them in true backwoods style. When Mrs. Moore came to the woods she was brought in an invalid; now with her husband she went hunting, fishing and guiding when there were ladies in the party.

"We came here to hunt and fish, my wife and I, and the less people come the better it will please us," said John Moore, as they were leaving in the morning. "But if the people will come we will try and take care of them in the proper season. It is past that now, so you can put up your money, I don't want it." Then they left the couple who cared for no society but their own and the wild free forests, with a friendly feeling in their hearts and the major part of two chickens in their knapsacks. These they needed before they got through the Indian Pass and on to Avalanche Lake, where they spent the night.

Here in 1868 occurred a pleasant little episode in which Bill Nye, a noted guide and hunter of North Elba, took a hand. Bill was one of those iron-molded men just turned fifty at the time, nearly six feet, powerfully built, knowing no danger or fatigue and well versed in woodcraft. Silent, morose if in any way you gained his dislike by a display of supposed superiority; but if he liked you he could not do too much for you. Always ready and willing, around the campfire his tongue would loosen and his stories were a sure cure for the blues.

His best-known story, the Hitch-up Matilda episode, was his most famous. "There were three other people involved — a Mr. and Mrs. Fielding and Dolly, their niece. Mr. Fielding was a small man, quick-motioned and impulsive. His wife was taller and heavier than he. The niece was about 17, a handsome girl who knew it too, very sociable and willing to talk to anyone.

"Well, on the way back to Placid from a trip to the Iron Works, we started to go through Avalanche Pass. You remember the walls, hundreds of feet high on either side. Along the west side is a shelf from two to four feet wide and about four feet under water that everybody don't know about. When we got there they wondered how we were going to get past. I said that I could either carry them or build a raft, but to make the raft would take some time while I could carry them over in a few minutes. Provisions were getting short and a definite time set to get back to North Elba, so Mr. Fielding says, 'Well, Matilda, what say you? Will you be carried across, or shall he make a raft?'

"Mrs. Fielding says, 'If Mr. Nye can do it and thinks it safe, I'll be carried over to save time.'

" 'Well, Dolly, what do you say?'

" 'Oh, if Mr. Nye can carry Aunt over he can *me*, of course, I think it would be a novelty.'

" 'Well,' said Mr. F., 'we have concluded to be carried over if you can do it safely.'

"I said, Perfectly safe, I once carried a man across who weighed 180 pounds and a nervous old fellow at that.

"So I first waded over and back to see if there had been a change in the bottom since I was there before. When in the deepest place the water is nearly up to my armpits for a step or two, but I had nothing with me then. When I got back Mrs. Fielding said that she did not see how I was going to carry them across and keep them out of the water.

"I said, I'll show you. Who is going to ride first?

"Mr. F. then said, 'It's politeness to see the ladies safe first, so Matilda must make the first trip.'

" 'Oh no!' she said, 'Let the politeness go. Mr. F. is to go over first!' But he insisted that she had agreed to ride if I said it was safe; now he wanted to see her do it.

"'So I will,' she said, 'How am I to do it?'

"I set down with my back against a rock that came nearly to the top of my shoulders, told her to step on the rock, put one foot over one side of my neck and the other foot over the other side and then sit down. *That* was what she did not feel inclined to do — she was going to climb on with both feet on one side. But her husband told her that she must throw away her

Hitch Up Matilda

59

squeamishness and do as I told her. He reminded her again of her word, which was enough. She finally set down, very carefully, but so far down my back that I could not carry her. I told her I couldn't do it. At last she got on right and I waded in.

" 'Hurrah, there they go!' and 'Cling tight, Matilda!' shouted the young lady and the husband in the same breath. 'Hold your horse, aunt!' laughed Dolly, 'Your reputation as a rider is at stake. Three cheers for Aunt Mazeppa! — I mean Aunt Matty — novel isn't it? Unique and pleasing. You'll beat Rarey, Auntie, that's what you'll do.'

"I had just got into the deep water and was steadying myself with one hand against the rocks and holding on to her feet with the other when, in spite of all I could do, she began to work down my back.

" 'Hitch up, Matilda, hitch up! Why don't you hitch up?' screamed Mr. Fielding. I could hear him dancing around the rocks and stones on the shore while I thought Dolly would have died laughing. And the more he yelled, 'Hitch up!' the more she hitched down and I began to think I would have to change ends. But by leaning way over forward, I managed to get her across safe and dry.

"Then she asked, 'How am I supposed to get off?' I'll show you, I said. So I got down 'til her feet touched the ground and she walked off over my head, the two on the other side laughing and shouting all the time.

"Then Dolly's turn; I told her that she must sit as straight as a major general. She said she would — she'd let them see that all the money spent at riding schools hadn't been thrown away in *her* case. Wondered if any poet would immortalize her as they had Phil Sheridan; then with some kind of a conundrum about Balaam (I never thought much of conundrums anyway) she got on and I took her over and unloaded her as I had her aunt.

"The rest was easy enough, rather more in my line too, and we got back all right. Of course I did no more than my duty at the time, but you can bet that I kept pretty still about it for some time. At last it leaked out, but there is one thing I would like to say: The ladies never made the slightest allusion to it in public — in my presence at least. And for that — showing so much regard for the feelings of a bachelor — I shall be grateful to my dying day."

From North Elba Stoddard and Oblenis trudged to Keene, that loveliest combination of quiet valley and wild mountain scenery to be found anywhere in the Adirondacks. There they met Orson Scofield (Old Mountain) Phelps some five years before Charles D. Warner immortalized him in his classic essay "The Primitive Man." Born in Vermont the guide, then 57 had an enthusiastic love for the woods, took to them at every opportunity and was a long time engaged in tracing out lot lines that extended far into the interior where, in those days, deer and speckled trout were as plentiful as mosquitoes on a damp day in July.

He didn't aspire to much as a hunter but claimed to have caught more trout than any other man in the country. In 1844 he was with Mr. Henderson at Adirondac, soon after which he married and settled in Keene Flats. In 1849 he made his first trip to the top of Marcy, passing over Haystack around the head of Panther Gorge to the summit, descending near where the main trail now runs; thus being the first man to get to the top from the east. He afterward cut what is now known as the Bartlett Mountain trail. Soon after that he guided two ladies up, which was considered quite a feat and a feather in his cap. He also marked trails to the top of Hopkins' Peak, the Giant, up John's Brook to Marcy, and several other trails. He also made a valuable map of the region around, was a prized and regular contributor to a local paper and wrote a voluminous treatise on the Adirondack lakes and mountains, trees, birds, beasts, etc., which showed the close observer and enthusiastic student of nature.

"We found him at his home near the falls that bear his name; a little old man about five feet six in height, muffled in an immense crop of long hair and beard that seemed to boil up out of his collarband. Grizzly as the granite ledges he climbs, shaggy as the rough-barked cedar, but with a pleasant twinkle in his eye and an elasticity to his step equaled by few younger men. He likes to talk and delivers his sage conclusions and whimsical oddities in a cheery, chirripy, squeaky sort of tone — away up on the mountains as it were — an octave above the ordinary voice, somewhat suggestive of the warbling of an ancient chickadee."

" 'So you wanted Old Mountain Phelps to show you the way, did you?' said he. 'Well, I 'spose I kin do it. I'll be along as soon as the old woman'll bake me a short cake. The wise man provides for a 'nermergency and hunger's one of 'em.'

"Old Mountain," rowed them to the other end of Lower Ausable; after a mile walk they reached the shore of Upper Ausable Pond, where Phelps expected to find his boat but didn't. " 'Just as I expected. Old Phelps' boat belongs to everybody but himself. Well, we haven't got much further to go to my shanty; that's one satisfaction, and maybe they'll let us stay there all night seeing that it belongs to me!"

Camp Phelps, where they stopped that night was, according to Stoddard's tongue-in-cheek description, one of the most complete in its appointments and management to be found anywhere in the mountains. "The structure is of an elegant design and built of magnificent logs cut and carved artistically with knots of various and unique patterns in bas-relief. The main door is about 2½ by 5 feet, swings outward and is locked with a string. It contains reception rooom, drawing room, private parlor and sleeping rooms en suite, with wardrobes sticking out all around the sides. The grand dining hall is situated out on the lawn, which is quite extensive, and furnished with hemlock extensions and stumps.

"This spacious structure is 6 by 10 feet on the ground, between 4 and 5 feet high and is surmounted by a Yankee roof of troughs in two layers; the upper layer is inverted, covering the crevices in the lower so as to exclude the rain, but separated far enough to give perfect ventilation. This chef d'oeuvre of architecture is luxuriously upholstered throughout with spruce boughs. In the culinary department is a stupendous range which floods the drawing room with light; in short, it contains all the modern improvements including hot and cold water, which is carried to every part of the establishment in pails.

"Here we gathered — Crawford's party of 7 and ours, 10 in all; besides there were 2 or 3 dogs, all of us in a space about 6 by 8 feet square. While the fire snapped and flickered, filling the shanty with dancing shadows, stories of hunting and fishing adventures were told that all were expected to believe because they were personal experiences. Occasionally though one of these would have a familiar sort of sound except for the names and dates. Stories of personal prowess were common and culminated in one of a man who could pick up a two-barrel iron kettle with his teeth. This feat was topped by the assertion of another guide, who claimed that he knew a man who could perform the same phenomenon while sitting in the kettle while he lifted it!

"These, however, were making light of serious subjects so Phelps told his bear story. One day near the Boreas he saw a big bear coming on the run and he was armed only with a little ax. But when the bear got within 20 feet of him, Orson yelled 'Halt!' This stopped the bear — then he wouldn't prevaricate, he did it with his little hatchet. He didn't feel scared any, only stared up like, but the bear reversed ends and made off as fast as it could wobble.

"Then Uncle Harvey (Holt) told about the time he had killed a bear once with a pitchfork and a moose with a club, after tiring him in the deep snow. 'But, by Gawl, boys,' he added, 'when Dick Estes tumbled over backwards on his snowshoes and the critter gave a lunge at him, I thought it was all up with him so I just gave command to the boys and at him we went. And by Gawl, the way we laid it on his hide was a caution! And there lay Dick, square on his back, looking up, thinkin' that every minute was his last. And by Gawl, I managed to get a lick at the critter that fetched him jest as he was standin' over Dick so!' Then the old hunter assumed a position indicative of an enraged moose preparing to come down on the unfortunate chap on his back in the snow, who couldn't turn over on account of his snowshoes.

"Thus each had his stories to tell until time to turn in, when four of the party went across the Pond to another camp. This left six of us to occupy a space six feet long by six feet wide where we slept on edge, like a box of well-packed sardines, until daylight. Then each man got up, cut a chunk of venison, salt pork or bacon as taste dictated and each one for himself waltzed around the stove in the six by ten shanty until he warmed it through enough to suit. Or, disguising pieces of raw material in an outside coating of bread, proceeded to stow it away with that appearance of keen enjoyment displayed by the average boy in taking a pill. Then some rushed away to put out the dogs while others went to the various runways

Ondawa House

to watch.

"After the others had gone Theo. White, another of the guides, came in with a bag of oatmeal which he made into pancakes. Three huge ones, the size of the frying pan but light as sea foam. Topped with maple sugar these cakes were to our hearts and stomachs like the blissful ecstasy of love's young dream."

After breakfast Phelps took them up to the inlet, with its dark borders of balsams and tamaracks, to the Marcy trail, where they bade him a regretful adieu for they had become attached to the cheery old man of the mountains. Then they started on their sixteen-mile trek through the woods past Mud (Elk) and Clear Lakes to Root's, on the Schroon Lake road. At that point they felt that they were now nearing friends and home again, clearer in thought and stronger in body than when they began the trip three weeks before. Glad to be going back to Glens Falls again but sad at the thought of leaving the mountains over which they saw the storm clouds gather, break and roll away, leaving them kissed by sunshine, clean, grand, strong and eternal as the hand that made them.

From Root's they took a stage to the Ondawa House at Schroon Lake, where John I. Filkins, the Albany Express robber had recently been captured. The town had apparently gone crazy over the subject of thief-taking so whenever a stranger showed himself there the class (and their name is legion) who have a perpetual contract for holding down chairs and squirting tobacco juice at and around the barroom stoves, resolved itself into a corps of detectives with self-delegated power to inquire into the antecedents of said strangers. At the same time the one duly authorized detective (!) was especially noticeable on account of his superior brilliancy and skill at "working up a case."

Such being the state of affairs it was not surprising that suspicion was excited when Stoddard and Oblenis registered and went in for a late supper.

"Soon an individual with expectation on his face and grease on his clothes opened the door, came part way in, then in a hesitating sort of way came entirely in and appeared to be looking for something which he evidently expected to find in the middle of the floor. Then in a mysterious manner he communed with the cook, who cleared a place at an adjoining table. Then when a lamp was brought, he seated himself and produced a newspaper which he spread out and over which he gazed intently at the hungry strangers.

"His mysterious actions were noticed and his uncertain manner set down as the modesty of a great soul who had come to spark the cook and been caught in the act, until he followed the gentlemen into the office to make some original and interesting remarks about the weather. Next, after spelling out the names on the register, he said:

" 'Wait a minute; I hope you will excuse me, but I want to look at your face.'

" 'Ah,' said the person appealed to, good-naturedly, while being gone over with a kerosene lamp; 'Somebody's wanted, and you represent the majesty of the law?'

"He modestly admitted that he had the honor of being 'constable.' "

" 'Well, who do you take me for?'

" 'I thought you might be the feller that stole some money at Ticonderoga, but you ain't.' Then he made another kerosene inspection and said he was satisfied, when anyone with half an optic could see that he was not. 'No, you ain't the one,' he said with a sigh as he sat down and felt of the stranger's boots, 'he had on Number 10 shoes.'

" 'Well, you're satisfied I hope!'

" 'Oh, I know you ain't the feller I want,' he said in a very decided way; then he made another thorough inspection. 'No, you ain't my man.' He went on with another sigh, 'for you haven't got a big scar on your right cheek, have you?' at the same time feeling of the cheek to satisfy himself that his eyes did not deceive him. After one or two more examinations the gifted man, when questioned, admitted that he was Darius Hill.

"Twice more this Argus-eyed representative of the law had attacks of uncertainty and had to satisfy himself. Then he left with the information that he did not feel called on to apologize, for 'his duty compelled him' etc., — and suggested that the matter be kept quiet, as too much publicity might ruin his chances of taking the actual thief.' "

The rest of the return trip was pleasant and uneventful.

Chapter 6

The Pictured Adirondacks

Although Stoddard was accorded considerable fame for his lectures based on his travels to distant parts of this country and abroad, he always insisted that his Adirondack programs were his best. The success of these lectures was undoubtedly due to his never-ending preference for the scenic delights of that alluring region of lakes, forests and hurrying streams which looms so enticingly on the northern horizon for anyone who lives in the Glens Falls-Lake George area. Apparently the attraction of the Adirondacks appealed not only to his artistic nature but also, as he intimated at both ends of the preceding chapter, they generated in him a deep awareness of and gratitude for their therapeutic benefits and values.

The first trip to the Adirondacks, which he cited in his conversation with Capt. Rockwell of the steamer "Vermont" seemingly did not result in many photographs even though it is known that in 1870 he saw the exceptionally photogenic deserted village of Adirondac and the nearby serrated High Peak sector. Pen and ink sketches and line drawings seem to have been the main delineative results of that journey.

On the second trip, however, Stoddard took numerous pictures which later won for him a reputation as a camera artist. These remarkable scenes, plus those taken on many later treks, provided him with superb visual effects for his lecture programs besides furnishing him with readily saleable views.

The 1873 trip took Stoddard through the most picturesque parts of the Adirondacks — Wilmington Notch and Whiteface Mountain, the North Elba — Lake Placid region, Paul Smith's on the St. Regis chain, Bartlett's and the Saranacs, the incomparable Keene Valley and the Ausables, the spectacular Indian Pass — Colden and Avalanche Lakes, the Marcy area, the Long, Blue Mountain and Raquette Lakes section. Although there were relatively few hotels in the mountains at that early period, most of those that had been built were caught on film. The guides of the era, undoubtedly the greatest the Adirondacks ever produced—Sabattis, Dunning and Phelps, plus Bill Nye, Paul Smith and Mart Moody — were per-

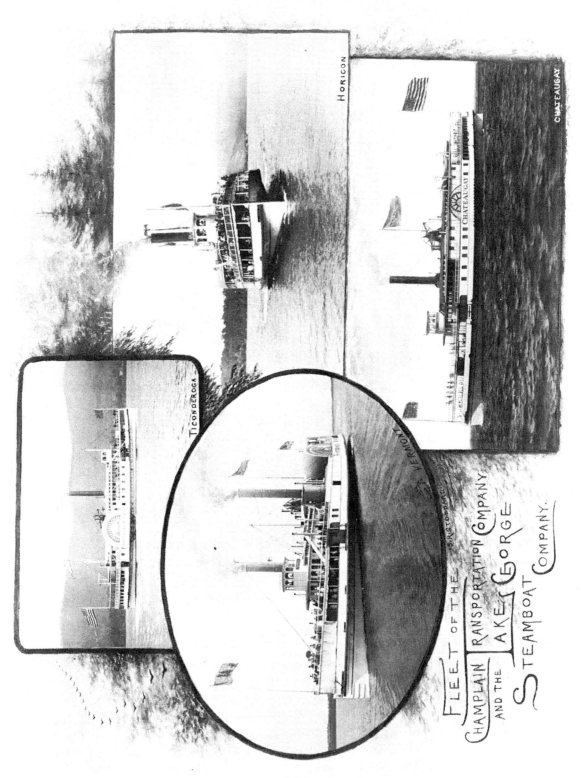

Fleet of the Champlain Transportation Company and the Lake George Steamboat Company.

HORICON

CHATEAUGAY

TICONDEROGA

VERMONT

Steamboat Fleet

66

Adirondack Railroad. Blue Mountain Lake.

67

Alvah Dunning

Old Mtn. Phelps

Mitchell Sabattis

Mart Moody

Bill Nye

Paul Smith

Composite of Guides

petuated by Stoddard prints. Never before nor after have the region's most memorable scenes and people been better or more thoroughly photographed.

Subsequent trips in 1876, 1877, 1878, 1879, during the 1880's and 1890's rounded out the impressive accumulation of prints for the Stoddard files. By then many more hotels had been built; steamboats were on nearly every sizeable lake and river. Guideboats and canoes were common on most navigable streams. Ornate lodges, less pretentious camps and cottages, and even lowly lean-tos (open camps) dotted the shores of many of the most and some of the least accessible bodies of water. The ubiquitous Stoddard — by railroad, boat, carriage, stagecoach or on foot — managed to see and photograph many if not most of these structures, their owners and guests and the water craft typical of the times.

While that amazingly energetic man was forever busy with his cameras, he was also making copious notes for his map and guidebook series. Never content with insufficient information, he and his guides penetrated practically every section of the Adirondack wilderness gathering the essential on-the-spot information which made his works the most authoritative examples of their types available to sportsmen and travelers.

Nor was he satisfied with merely reprinting or rehashing the results of a single trip and letting it go at that, as so many other so-called Adirondack authorities did. By 1900 he had visited not once but several times many of the most remote regions of the mountains from the Chateaugay Lakes on the north to the southern foothills below Honnedaga, from the western shore of Lake Champlain to the distant valley of the St. Lawrence. Small wonder then that people who best knew the mountains placed so much well-warranted confidence in and derived so much pleasure from the work of Stoddard.

Although the maps and guidebooks complemented S. R. Stoddard's fame as a photographer, his greatest contribution to posterity was undoubtedly the pictures themselves. The best of these he painstakingly tinted and used to enhance his lectures. These popular programs were given in towns and cities all along the Eastern seaboard from Massachusetts to Florida and entranced audiences from West Virginia to Nebraska.

The versatile Stoddard used several titles for these Adirondack programs and varied his material according to the location of the place where he was appearing. Usually the lecture content featured the Adirondack region proper, but he usually included scenes which had more local appeal. For the people in towns north of the Mohawk the program generally concluded with views of Albany. For Hudson Valley and New York audiences views of that majestic river, West Point, the Palisades, the Harbor and the Statue of Liberty were sure to be shown. For residents of Rochester and Buffalo the lecturer added the renowned visual attractions of Niagara Falls by sunlight and moonlight.

It is quite understandable, therefore, why the lecturer changed his titles from time to time. In some cities the program was called "The Pictured Adirondacks;" elsewhere it was billed as the "Illustrated Adirondacks." Still another lecture traced in verse the Hudson from its source to the sea. This was called either by that name or as "The Hudson River from the Mountains to the Sea." But whatever he called it, his talk invariably was accompanied by some 225 delicately-tinted lantern slides projected on a canvas screen which measured 30 by 30 feet.

Unquestionably the most important as well as the most effective of Stoddard's lectures on the Adirondack theme was the one that he delivered in the Assembly chamber at Albany on February 25, 1892. A reporter for the Albany *Evening Journal* sent in the following account the next day:

"The Assembly chamber last evening, instead of serving as a place wherein the laws of the State are conceived, was turned into an exhibition hall and one of the best — if not the best — illustrated lectures ever given in this city was rendered by S. R. Stoddard of Glens Falls. Long before 8 o'clock every available seat was taken and many were left standing. The fame of Mr. Stoddard and his wonderful collection of views of Adirondack scenery having preceded him had called together the large audience.

"The lecture was primarily for the purpose of showing to the public that great and beautiful natural park to the north of us, to the end that the interests of the people might be awakened to the idea of protecting the forest and keeping it in its natural condition.

"As the entertainment was under the direction of the State Forestry Commission, the president of that body, Townsend Cox, in introducing the lecturer, thanked the people for their presence and explained that the purpose of the meeting was that a bill might be passed by the Legislature creating an Adirondack Park. He said that everyone should be interested in that project because the Adirondacks were not for the few but for all the people.

"The lecturer first caused to be thrown upon the screen a map showing what he termed the gateways to the Adirondacks. He then took his hearers through each gateway, explaining the principal points of interest along each route.

"He said that the Adirondack region proper is all included in about 100 square miles, although the term has, by established use, come to include a tract of about 8,000 square miles; the greater part of this area lies to the west of the great peaks on a plateau which averages about 1600 feet above tide water, and is known as the lake region. The Wilderness is divided into three general divisions — the mountain region which is best approached from Westport; the northern lake region, which is commonly entered via the Chateaugay Railroad, and the southwest lake region, which includes Blue Mountain, Raquette and Long Lakes and which is accessible from Saratoga by the Adirondack Railroad.

"Probably two-thirds of the visitors enter the wilderness from the east

Trudeau Sanitarium patients

and it is also probable that at least one-third do so by way of the Chateaugay Railroad and Plattsburgh.

"Beginning with views of the Lake Champlain region the lecturer took his audience for a most interesting trip, the mind's eye being materially assisted by the very vivid pictures of lake and mountain scenes thrown upon the screen.

"The armchair tourists were first taken to Saranac Lake where, among other interesting views, were those of the Adirondack Sanitarium (Trudeau's), showing patients wrapped up in furs sitting on the verandas, the picture having been taken in January.

"Excellent pictures of the Saranac Lake hotels were shown, and here Mr. Stoddard remarked that the Adirondacks contain between 150 and 160 hotels whose rates range from $1.00 to $4.00 per day and whose total capacity is about 5,000 guests.

"Other interesting pictures were a camp interior, pictures of Adirondack boats and portraits of typical guides. The 'travelers' were then taken to Upper Saranac Lake; next on a trip to Paul Smith's and then up the Raquette River to Tupper Lake.

Wawbeek, Upper Saranac Lake

Saranac Lake Hotel compo

*Prospect House
Later Saranac Inn*

Berkeley Hotel, Saranac Lake

Ampersand
Lower Lake

Martin's
Later — Miller's
Lower Lake

Alexander
Later
Algonquin
Lower Lake

Camp Stott, Raquette Lake — interior scene

Drowned Lands of the Lower Raquette

"The selfish policy of the lumbermen who, by erecting dams for mill and timber-driving purposes, flooded a large level tract in what was originally one of the most beautiful valleys in the mountains and thereby created the so-called drowned lands of the Raquette, was dwelt upon at some length by the speaker.

"Views of Lake Placid, the summit of Whiteface Mountain, the grave of old John Brown, and a number of Adirondack lodges proved of much interest. The cost of one of these structures, Pine Knot on Raquette Lake, owned by W. W. Durant, was said to have been more than $50,000. Then a series of views of legendary Indian Pass, Lake Colden and Avalanche Lake, said to be the wildest section in the whole territory, was shown.

"The lecturer next read a very creditable original poem describing the course of the Hudson River from its source in tiny Lake Tear of the Clouds, the most elevated body of water in the state, to the sea. The poem was illustrated by some of the finest views of the entire collection and included quite a number of local interest. Pictures of state officers and legislators were also shown. The lecture closed with views of New York City and the harbor."

Raquette Lake, Camp Pine Knot

Indian Pass, south from summit rock

*Avalanche Lake
from the North*

76

Lake Tear of the Clouds

Ausable Lakes

A reporter for another Albany paper, The *Argus,* added still more graphic details. "A bewitching picture of a summer girl was thrown upon the canvas, accompanied by the lecturer's statement that ladies make the tour of the Adirondacks in couples accompanied only by their guides. The Adirondacks have no vicious characters as visitors and there are no venomous reptiles throughout the mountain region proper.

"Ausable Lake, Lower Ausable Lake and the region roundabout received attention. Lower Ausable is Swiss-like in its beauty and combines more points of loveliness than any other lake in the northern wilderness.

"Beautiful flashlight photographs were shown, depicting open camps with fires burning in front of them. . . . Pictures were shown of trim little steamers running through shallow streams into Raquette Lake. Mr. Stoddard said that when he first visited the section in 1870 there was but one person living in all this region. He was a squatter on an island who subsisted by hunting and fishing. It was old Alvah Dunning, whose picture was shown.

"Through the Fulton Chain of eight lakes the lecture ran, finally returning to the central mountain peak, Mt. Marcy. Another map was projected giving the location of the proposed State Park which is to contain about 4,000 square miles. Within that territory the State actually owns only about 800 square miles, while private associations own 2,000 miles of de-

Between Blue Mountain and Eagle Lake

78

sirable preserve. The remainder is controlled by lumbermen. The Hudson River drains about a third of the Adirondack region and the rest of the territory is part of the St. Lawrence watershed system. Mr. Stoddard declared that if he had the power he would pass a law which stipulated that no evergreen tree should be cut on land 1,500 feet above tide unless under the supervision of competent persons and with the approval of qualified state officials . . .

"The course and growth of the Hudson from its beginning as a rivulet far up in the woods was described with its wanderings along by hunters' camps, surveyors' shacks, woodsmen's and log-choppers' shanties. The snow scenes and bits of landscape were exquisite.

"Evidently the law-makers who saw this program were greatly impressed by it and it is hoped that it will have a salutary effect on the legislation which will be considered this season."

The same program was repeated in many of the larger cities of the state during the next three months. A reporter for the Rochester *Herald* (April 25, 1892) expressed his reaction in the following excerpt from the lecture given at the Music Hall under the auspices of the Genesee Valley Forestry Association: "Mr. Stoddard's pictures showed the natural beauty of regions unmarred by the desecrating axes of the lumbermen in contrast to the bare and wasted tracts visited by them. The devastating and dismal effects of denuding the mountain slopes of their protecting growths of trees was described in a way so lucid as to present in a convincing manner to the hearers the necessity and advantage of prompt action by the State in protecting these regions from further spoliation.

"As a protective measure the passage of an act restricting the cutting of trees above a certain elevation (1500 feet above tide) was suggested. The speaker asserted that action in the matter must come from people outside the Adirondack region, where the inhabitants are comparatively indifferent, from people anxious to preserve for the State the charm of its most beautiful sections.

" 'Illustrated Adirondacks' as presented by Mr. Stoddard is an entertainment that cannot be too often heard and seen in various parts of this State. It entertains, interests and instructs all persons who attend it. It also presents the facts and actual conditions of a state of affairs whose evils are too little known and whose only remedy is the successful agitation of the public mind by just such methods and means as those which constitute Mr. Stoddard's 'Illustrated Adirondacks.' "

An editorial writer for the Newburgh *Daily News* called the program "A grand panorama of the Adirondacks, a vast region which is yearly becoming more familiar to thousands of the lovers of nature and the outdoor life. The stereopticon brought out the charms and beauties of valley and mountain, lake and river to the full. As the pictures seemingly chased each other across the canvas, the lecturer kept up a running fire of comment and explanation of which his audience never wearied. One seemed to breathe

the pure mountain air, fragrant with the balmy odors of pine and spruce, and to see in reality the clear, sparkling water, the dense forests, the grassy slopes and revel in natural scenery unsullied by the hand of man."

Then followed the hard-hitting verbal and pictorial attack on ruthless lumbering practices cited in the preceding account.

The New York *Times* printed the following reaction to a similar lecture given at Chickering Hall on April 27, 1892. "A large audience followed the discourse with interest and frequently expressed appreciation of the beautiful and artistic colored views which were thrown upon the huge screen. While providing an entertainment of a most enjoyable nature, Mr. Stoddard's object is also to call attention to the actual conditions, occupancy and needs of the lovely district of the Upper Hudson. Graphic pictures of romantic camps, views of hunting and fishing scenes were enough to whet the appetite of even the most indolent of sportsmen.

"But," said Mr. Stoddard, "it is not just to kill either game or time that people need care to spend a little while in the Adirondacks. All who love the sublime and majestic in nature or the dainty and beautiful scenery of lake and woodland will find here, within easy reach, a variety which is charming and a peaceful grandeur which must soothe and elevate their weary minds. . . .

"The despoiling work of man was amply illustrated by views of flooded lands covered with dead timber, and the lecturer's appeal for the preservation of this charming wilderness was powerful.

"Mr. Stoddard handled his subject in a most entertaining manner. His delivery was clear, explicit and persuasive."

A Glens Falls *Daily Times* writer remarked "If the lecture as delivered by Mr. Stoddard last evening (May 9, 1892), with the accompanying illustrations, could be attended generally throughout the State, it would do more in two months' time to correct the abuses of the Adirondacks than all the surveys and commissions of the past twenty years."

On May 20th, the long-awaited vote on the bill to establish the Adirondack Park was passed by the Legislature and signed by Gov. Hill. Apparently what S. R. Stoddard had shown to many of the legislators and their constituents had produced its desired effect. Not that he claimed the lion's share of the credit because he was not that sort of person, but it is significant and noteworthy that the organizations and the individuals who had led the long and bitter battle to establish the Park were quick to express their praise and gratitude for his timely and valued services.

Although most of Stoddard's lectures were scheduled during the winter season, he nevertheless took full advantage of the opportunities presented by the summer resorts as well. According to various issues of *The Summer Resorter* and the *Adirondack News* which came out during the mid 1890's, he often entertained at the better-known Adirondack hotels. Besides the lecture itself he had available for sale pictures of various sizes. While some of these were of the stereopticon type and therefore sold singly, representative views of a particular area were usually bound together as albums.[1]

His Books of Pictures, as he called them, generally had twelve 10 x 12 inch photogravure plates. Bound in torchon board with illuminated titles, these were captioned as follows: *Among the Mountains of the Adirondacks, Through the Lake Country of the Adirondacks, The Hudson River from its Source to the Sea* and *Ausable Chasm*.

Another album, which he called *Souvenirs of the North*, contained 18 to 30 selected 5½ x 7 inch views of Blue Mountain Lake, Raquette Lake, Long Lake, Tupper Lake region; *Wild Lakes of the Adirondacks* (Ausable, Avalanche, Colden, Tear of the Clouds, Sanford, Henderson, etc.); *Elizabethtown and Keene Valley, North Elba and beyond Lake Placid, the Saranac Lakes, Winter at Saranac Lake* and other resorts outside the Adirondacks.

Avalanche Pass

---

1. In addition to brisk sales of photos, Stoddard also published hotel brochures, stationery and scenic postcards both black and white and tinted. He was a pioneer in the latter field.

There were still other larger albums respectively called *Bits of Adirondack Life, The Adirondack Mountains Illustrated, Camp Life* and *Picturesque Adirondack Resorts.* The last, his deluxe item, measured 11 x 14 inches and featured composite phototype views of the Adirondacks, Lake George and Lake Champlain.

Besides these albums Stoddard also published his *Photographs of New York Scenery.* This took the form of an illustrated volume which contained a thousand subjects, printed in clusters of 25 each, grouped according to subject and numbered to correspond with the accompanying descriptive catalog. The resulting montage or composite gave in miniature, one-fifth its original size, what he considered to be every important picture in the series, and included the following sequences: The Hudson from its Source to the Sea, Saratoga, Lake George, Lake Champlain, Ausable Chasm and the Adirondack Wilderness.

The official photographer for the American Canoe Association, Stoddard also held the same position with both the Delaware and Hudson and the Adirondack Railroad (Saratoga to North Creek).

However impressed a person may be with both the quality and the quantity of the Stoddard Adirondack views in particular, only those people who have stood on the exact spots where these pictures were taken can really appreciate them. This is especially true of the Indian Pass and Marcy scenes. Even today anyone who wends his usually weary way up through that awesome Pass from the south finds the going quite strenuous at times. The steep ledges, the massive boulders, the feet-entangling tree roots, the slippery footing—all these make that trail, particularly when one is laden with a heavy pack, a somewhat tiresome stint even for the hardiest hiker.

Not that Stoddard personally toted all the bulky paraphernalia; the guides lugged most of that — the heavy tripod, the bulky cameras, the weighty boxes of wet plates, the bottles of collodion and chemicals, etc. But, even though the party otherwise traveled light and lived off the land as much as possible, there were still guns and well-loaded packbaskets to be carried and the photographer was never known to shirk from doing his share of the work.

Stoddard's Adirondack scenes are in a class by themselves because they possess today, just as they did three short generations ago, pronounced pictorial and historical values. His most noteworthy bequest to his contemporaries and to us was a priceless heritage — his photographic and pictorial record of Adirondack yesteryears.

Chapter 7

Stoddard's Night Pictures

Superb photographic skill was shown by S. R. Stoddard in his daylight scenes but even more extraordinary were his moonlight and after dark effects. Among his masterpieces were those taken in the Adirondacks; in New York, Chicago and in cities abroad, such as Paris, London and

The Antlers, Open Camp, Raquette Lake

Athens. Some of the most outstanding mountain pictures caught on film featured the clouds, rippling water and silhouetted mountains and evergreens of Long and Blue Mountain Lakes and Lake George. But even more exceptional and fascinating were the campfire photographs.

Judging by the number of each which were produced, the most popular of the flash scenes were those showing groups in front of the oversized open camps at the Sagamore on Long Lake; Camp Phelps on Upper Ausable Lake; Under the Hemlocks, C. H. Bennett's world-famed resort on Raquette Lake and at spacious Adirondack Lodge during its legendary heyday under the fabulous Mr. Van (Henry van Hoevenbergh).

To many, however, the most memorable were those which recorded for posterity the railroad survey party at Long Lake in 1888, the firelight composition called "Adirondack Hunters" and the one variously called "Big Game in the Adirondacks" and "Wild Adirondack Game."

Besides their obvious pictorial values these photographs have historical significance as well. The size, shape and structure of the lean-

Story telling around the Campfire — Adirondack Lodge

Henry van Hoevenbergh (Mr. "Van")

Adirondack Survey party at Long Lake 1888

tos (open camps) and lodges, the clothing and props worn or used by the people pictured, the preponderance of bearded or mustachioed men, their general appearance and facial expressions — these and other such details are of considerable significance to the historically-minded as well as to the professionals in this field.

Incidentally, as any careful observer will notice, the campfire flames were dubbed in later during the developing process.

This raises a question of somewhat more than passing interest to the ever-increasing millions of people who practice photography. Just how were these unusual pictures taken, what techniques were used, how could facial expressions be so startlingly clear? Good questions when one also takes into consideration the fact that these scenes were dated 1878, 1882 or 1889.

The photography editor of the New York *Daily Tribune* was also interested in just such questions. On March 2, 1890 his correspondence with Stoddard appeared in the paper which the great Horace Greeley founded. Believing that many readers would like to know some of the technical details involved, the editor wrote a rather lengthy article on the subject. This interview, which fills one and three-fourths columns, was entitled "Wonders of Flashlight Photography" and disclosed the following information concerning that phase of picture-taking in general and Stoddard's techniques and innovations in particular:

"New York Daily Tribune

Sunday, March 2, 1890

WONDERS OF FLASHLIGHT PHOTOGRAPHY

Some of the Things Accomplished

"Photography has made wonderful progress within the last few years. With the introduction of gelatine dry-plates, about ten years ago, the processes necessary to take a finished photograph were greatly simplified and cheapened. As a result, a great impetus was given photography; it being widely adopted by people of leisure, both men and women, as a pastime. Soon, however, it became a more serious occupation with amateurs. Highly-educated people, especially those scientifically inclined, took it up as an aid to other studies, and later, for the sake of developing the fascinating art itself. Everyone knows how the charming recreation has grown in popularity. There are thousands of amateur photographers in this country, and over a hundred photographic societies.

"Before the introduction of the modern gelatine dry-plate there were few, if any, amateur photographers. It required a complicated and tedious process to make a photograph in those days. The collodion emulsion or 'wet' process which was used made necessary cumbersome and costly apparatus; and it required at least ten seconds, under the most favorable circumstances of light and atmosphere, to make a picture in the field. Now, good photographs can be made in the hundredth and even the thousandth

Big Game in the Adirondacks

part of a second. It is not even necessary to have daylight to make good photographs in the fraction of a second; for burning magnesium metal, which was introduced as a new source of actinic or photographic light by Gaedike and Meithe, German chemists, in 1887, has made it possible for photographers to dispense with the rays of Old Sol. Instantaneous photographs by magnesium 'flash' light can now be made at home in the evening; in the theatre or lecture-room, and out of doors in the open night, or in caves, mines and other dark places.

Recent Achievements

"The latest achievements in the line of photographing by means of burning magnesium metal are those made by S. R. Stoddard, of Glens Falls, who has successfully photographed at night immense subjects like the Washington Memorial Arch and the Statue of Liberty Enlightening the World.

"The Washington Memorial Arch was his first attempt, and in photographing it he came near losing his life, for the unusually large amount of magnesium metal which he employed to illuminate the subject 'instead of boiling up out of the cup, as any well-mannered charge ought to have done, and as guncotton and gunpowder charges heretofore had always been in the habit of doing with me' he writes, 'the force of this one seemed to be downward, like dynamite, exploding with a loud detonation, tearing the cup into fragments and boiling down over my head and shoulders in a sheet of flame that singed hair and beard, and seared my hands and the side of my face as with a hot iron so that after I had got my slide in and saved my plate, I held an impromptu reception of policemen and a sympathetic crowd generally, followed by a free ride in an ambulance to St. Vincent's. But the photograph was entirely successful!!'

"It will be remembered how the photograph of Liberty Enlightening the World was made; that was a more recent achievement. Mr. Stoddard employed five instruments on this occasion, stationing them on the steamboat pier of the island, so that if he failed in one he would have four other chances. A wire was stretched from the torch of the big statue to the mast of a vessel a considerable distance away. Meanwhile, on this wire, and controlled by a pulley, was the magnesium compound to the electric plant on the island, so that at a given signal the electrician who had charge of the torch could turn on the current and produce a spark in the magnesium compound that would suddenly ignite it into a brilliant flash. Over a pound and a half of the magnesium was used, the largest quantity that was ever employed at one time in making a photograph. And this was also entirely successful.

Scenes in the Mountains

"Mr. Stoddard has made some remarkable photographs at night, by the magnesium "flash" light, in the Adirondacks, of camping scenes and life in the woods. One picture, which shows a group of hunters about a campfire, with a number of fine bucks hung up in a conspicuous place, is especially interesting. Another shows a number of bats photographed by magnesium light as they hung on the walls of Howe's Cave. 'The bats of Howe's Cave are not ordinary bats,' says Mr. Stoddard. 'I am not naturalist enough to tell wherein they differ from other bats, but that they do is certain, for they have been the subject of special study by learned professors, who reveled in vermin generally, and cut up bugs and things to see how they are made; they cling onto the rocks by their hind legs, and no amount of argument can make them understand the risk they run of apoplexy by so doing. I had placed my camera in position and focused on a lighted match held there, bringing the lens to about the same distance from the rock as the ground glass was back of the lens, that I might make the bats appear life-size. When all was ready I ignited about a quarter of an ounce of "flash" powder close to the side of the camera, and to make more certain of success, exposed a second plate in like manner.' . . . . ."

One of the most popular lectures in Stoddard's repertory was advertised as "The Wonderful White City of '93," which was later shortened to "The White City." Chicago in that year was the host city of the great Columbian Exposition or World's Fair and it gave the photographer from

Washington Square Arch N.Y.C.

Statue of Liberty

Adirondack Hunters

Glens Falls unlimited scope to parade his skill with the Kodak. The co-operative management placed all their facilities at his disposal so S.R.S. had a proverbial field day.

The results, after they had been colored by A. G. Marshall of Cazenovia under Stoddard's supervision, were apparently nothing short of spectacular. Using a dissolving view stereopticon lantern which projected by means of oxyhydrogen light an image which filled a canvas screen which measured nearly 1,000 square feet, the slide series must have been sensational. Proof of this are the words of a reporter for the Brooklyn *Citizen* of Feb. 10, 1894:

"The most interesting entertainment ever held in Bensonhurst was that of the New York Canoe Club at Bensonhurst Hall last evening. Mr. S. R. Stoddard presented about 150 of the most marvelous stereopticon views ever shown here. His World's Fair scenes were of a most startling reality. The White City alight with electricity was once more vividly brought before those who had attended the Fair. Those who had not were dumbfounded with the vastness of the place. Mr. Stoddard talked with a simplicity of language and an ease which was more like a storyteller than a lecturer.

"Among the illustrations were most of the principal buildings and thoroughfares, all of which were preceded by three or four introductory ones — the coming of the Viking Ship, the Spanish caravels, America (which was represented by the Statue of Liberty, of which view Mr. Bartholdi, its maker, has described as being the only one he ever saw worthy of the subject). Also the infant Chicago and a bit of the great city of today were shown. Then followed scenes depicting the lakefront, a glimpse of the White City, a mushroom street within the gates. Next came a long series of scenes so lifelike that the people appeared to be moving about and all perfectly recognizable if any friend happened to be in the audience.

"One of the most wonderful views was of the Ferris Wheel from different angles, showing the great mechanism as a whole and then separate portions of it. Mr. Stoddard showed Alaska at the Fair and then the Eskimo at home, which was an interesting comparison. An ostrich farm, the Orient and the Occident, Egyptian wedding processions, Soudanese and Nubian dancers, a royal mummy (not the Queen!) etc., were some of the diversions.

"Other after-dark effects showed the spotlighted buildings and the fascinating play of colored lights on the statues, the buildings and the waters of the lake and fountains. There was not an ordinary one among the whole series shown and although the White City is now no more, such mementoes of it will live forever."

Reports on this same program when it was later shown in other cities and towns were of the same highly complimentary nature. All of these — and there are many clippings to confirm this universally favorable reaction — are eloquent testimonials to Stoddard's exceptional ability to take unforgettable pictures at night as well as in the sunlight.

He was equally successful with his evening views of Gibraltar, the Alhambra, the Acropolis, the Sphinx, the Eiffel Tower, the Arc de Triomphe, St. Peters and other classic subjects in Europe, the Midnight Sun, the Near East and North Africa.

Chapter 8

The Cruise of the Canoe "Atlantis"

The following article from the Glens Falls *Republican* of June 22, 1886 furnishes the basic information about one of the most interesting and adventurous canoe trips ever attempted. It was also a venture that very nearly ended in tragedy several times during the voyage.

"This year S. R. Stoddard of this place expects to complete his canoe voyage begun in 1883. He started from here on August 7th of that year and part of the way his craft was towed. When he left here it was not his purpose to journey entirely in the "Atlantis," but to use it as a tender, and he expected to use the regular transportation from place to place. However, upon reaching New York he found the prevailing idea was that his contemplated excursion was to be made solely in the canoe. Lest he be accused of weakness or timidity, he decided not to back out so on August 9th, accompanied by Charles Oblenis, he sailed from the Battery.

"They proceeded as far as Vineyard Sound, where the trip ended for the season. The next year, accompanied by R. B. Burchard of New York, son of the minister of three R's notoriety, he continued his cruise, finishing for the season at Bar Harbor, Maine. Last summer the two completed the third stage of their journey which ended at St. John, New Brunswick. This year it is purposed to go from that city to the head of the Bay of Fundy where the bold canoeists will visit Acadia, the scene of Longfellow's "Evangeline."

"The longest canoe excursion on record is that of N. H. Bishop, a distance of 2,500 miles in 1874-5, but the itinerary he used skirted the open Atlantic (St. Lawrence River — Richelieu River — Lake Champlain — Hudson River — Raritan River — canal route to Philadelphia — Delaware River and Bay — along Atlantic coast to Charleston, then to Savannah — Savannah River to Florida — then descent of the St. Mary's River and portage to the Suwanee and down it to Gulf of Mexico) and was not so difficult or dangerous to sail.

"When the Atlantis has finished her long journey Mr. Stoddard will be able to feel gratified that he has sailed the entire distance, little less than 2,000 miles, every foot of the way in the smallest craft that ever sailed the whole length of the New England coastline. Mr. Stoddard will leave New York today to confer with Mr. Burchard and plan the remainder of the trip."

The casual, matter-of-fact coverage did of course provide the basic facts concerning the cruise, but it left out the exciting and almost fatal incidents which very nearly brought the risky voyage to a sudden watery conclusion on several occasions. But before those dramatic highpoints were reached it is necessary that we learn how such an idea took shape in the first place. Stoddard himself furnished that information because he wrote a two-volume, cleverly and profusely illustrated account of the journey in 1890.

His friend, the same N. H. Bishop, had written up his trip from Quebec to the Gulf in a book entitled "The Voyage of the Paper Canoe."[1] That account fired Stoddard with emulative zeal — but with a different destination. Bishop had sailed to the land of unfailing summer, so S. R. decided to push toward the region of perpetual ice. Bishop had gone alone; gregarious Stoddard wanted a companion.

Not as imbued with the yen for canoeing as he might have been, he looked upon the projected trip not so much as a cruise but as a trip made more practicable and pleasant by having a canoe along. His original plan was to go down the Hudson River, then eastward through Long Island Sound, over and around Cape Cod, up the coast to the head of the Bay of Fundy, then cross over to the Gulf of St. Lawrence, thence up that river to Montreal, then through the Richelieu River and Lake Champlain and via the canal back to Glens Falls. En route he would be pledged to no time or place, but go as the wind listeth and stop at Fancy's call. He wanted to visit places dear to history. "I would stand on Cape Cod's drifting sands. I would find shelter as did the Pilgrims of old where its encircling rim holds ancient Provincetown. I would stand where stood Leif Ericson and his hardy Norsemen 500 years before the country was officially discovered by Columbus. I would breathe the aromatic odors from the nutmeg groves of Connecticut; grapple with the wildest of Earth's known tides and with thick fogs on the Bay of Fundy and rest me in far Acadia, the home of Evangeline.

"There would be no prescribed rule of transit. It was to be for recreation — not to do penance — a search over a variable course for scene and incident. Conventional ways were to be prescribed but anything that promised variety would be welcome: a lumber ship from the Provinces; a coaler from the south, a cod-fisher from the Banks; a pinkie, a periauger or a Chinese junk. The Canoe was to be the connecting link between such possible craft — a means of reaching out-of-the way places, where native simplicity had not suffered from the blighting visit of the tourist and

1. Lee & Shepard. Boston, 1878

where the stranger was not looked upon simply as game to be mercilessly plucked."

He studied all available authorities for the perfect model of a canoe that would carry two people comfortably with their bedding, blankets, clothing and enough provisions to sustain life for a reasonable period. It had to be able to live in rough water and also carry all the appliances for safety that ingenuity could devise and space permit. Finally, after haunting boatyards for weeks, he gave up and set about whittling out his own model. This completed he took it to Joyner,[1] an experienced Adirondack guideboat maker who was also an original thinker and inventor whose innovations were frequently and dishonestly copied. Therefore, he had become suspicious of everyone and constantly carried a chip on his shoulder.

Stoddard went to him, explained his plans and got the following reactions:

"You don't want a canoe for that trip," said he, assuming command at once. "What you want is just a sail and rowboat combined — an Irene model!"

"No," I explained, "I want a canoe."

"No you don't either; 'tain't safe; you want just what I say!" — and the shoulder with the chip on it swung around aggressively.

"But I have made up my mind," I continued sweetly, "that for this trip I want a canoe!"

"I say you don't — might as well commit suicide at once and be done with it."

"Well, I propose to start anyway and if you won't fit one out someone else will."

Joyner glared at me a moment in silence then said, "Well, demmit, what kind of a thing do you want anyway?"

"I want a canoe built after my own model."

"Huh!"

"Well?"

"Bet you a dollar, if you dare, you won't get to Cape Cod alive and if you don't go to the bottom the first time that you strike salt water, I'll be mightily mistaken!" Such was the closing gun of the engagement.

Eventually the old boat-builder entered into the spirit of the enterprise with enthusiasm and he turned out a magnificent copy of the smaller prototype. Whatever was faulty he assigned to the designer; whatever was good Joyner just smiled and looked knowingly.[2] The finished product — a stiff, swift and dry boat — was eighteen feet long and three feet wide,

---

1. Fletcher Joyner, of Glen Lake and, later, Schenectady, won international fame for himself and E. H. Barney, who sailed their "Pecowsic 3" to resounding victories at the 1886 American Canoe Association regatta and elsewhere.

2. Stoddard was cited by both C. Vaux (*Canoe Handling*) and W. P. Stephen (*Canoe and Boat Building*) for his inventions and innovations in sails and rigging.

twenty-four inches high at bow, twenty at stern and fourteen amidships. She carried 150 feet of cloth in two sails besides oars and paddles. A firm deck covered all but the open cockpit, which was seven feet long and twenty-seven inches wide. A coaming four inches high surrounded this opening, and a water-tight canvas, fitted to button down tight around its edges with a bag-like opening after to gather up the body, was designed to keep out flying spray or pelting storm. A small tent, to be strung between the masts at night, covered the cockpit where they slept. Blankets, pillows and extra clothing were kept in water-tight bags and were utilized as seats, or stowed forward under the deck when not needed. Canned fruits and meats with oatmeal and kindred things in tin boxes with screw tops, served as ballast. Books, charts, photographs, dry plates and such small articles were kept free from moisture by being stowed in a compartment with an alleged water-tight hatch. Other compartments, hermetically sealed, occupied space at bow and stern and were designed to float the canoe and its occupants in case of an upset or capsizing.

Some years before the building of the "Atlantis" Stoddard had become half-owner of two boys. They were just common-sized boys, named LeRoy aged 7 and Charles (Bert) aged 13, but somehow they managed to fill up all the space on his grounds and occasionally boiled over into adjoining territory. They were given to noise and fun and were no end of trouble but on the whole, they fairly paid their way except in an off year and he thanked the Lord for them.

The two sons acted as his crew on the maiden voyage from Glens Falls down the feeder canel to Ft. Edward, Ft. Miller, Mechanicville, along the Hudson from Waterford to Albany. There he left the "Atlantis" at the Mohican Canoe Club and took his sons home to Glens Falls.

First Stage Cruise of the Atlantis

A short time later S. R. and Charles Oblenis, who had been his Adirondack hiking companion ten years previously, left Albany behind them and headed south down the storied Hudson. Given several assists by passing tows (tugboats pulling barges) they had a leisurely trip down-river. After a short stay at Nyack (former home of Oblenis), the two travelers were caught in a sudden squall in the Tappan Zee which nearly ended them and the trip simultaneously. The little craft was spared when the wind fortunately subsided and they had a chance to bail her out. They sailed the rest of the way to their next destination, the Knickerbocker Canoe Club at the foot of 85th Street, and there spent the night.

The next morning several reporters appeared and right then Stoddard found out that through a misunderstanding, they had been written up in the New York papers as two foolhardy canoeists bound on a two-thousand-mile voyage. The predicament was great but the companions decided that since it was a matter of pride and that there had been sizable bets made as to how far the "Atlantis" would go before foundering, there was only one thing to do — stick with the canoe as far as she would take them. Later, two members of the New York Canoe Club also put in their appearance and spent the rest of the night with them.

By ten the following morning the "Atlantis" had rounded the Battery and headed east through Hell Gate and on to Milton Harbor, where they went aground on a mud bank temporarily but then they were helped out by an obliging man who recognized the little boat from the newspaper description. The next morning the tide set them free and they made it over the tricky Fairfield Bar and on toward Bridgeport. Just outside that harbor they were caught between a pleasure sloop and a tugboat with a schooner in tow. The fun-loving captains of these two vessels crowded the "Atlantis" onto the shallow flats, where the breakers were rolling high. They finally managed to get her on an even keel again after she had been nearly swamped by the high waves, but they wrecked a sail and the steering gear in the process of getting into the Bridgeport anchorage.

Repairs made the next day they went on to the Thimble Islands, where they were the main attraction at the "best hotel." The following day they covered 35 miles and landed at Osprey Beach near New London. From that place on they were nearing the open sea and dangerous Point Judith, which they were to avoid that day by taking shelter behind Watch Hill. They decided to go on anyhow and found themselves contending with the might and majesty of the mountainous waves. After some anxious hours of being tossed about in the chop, they slid into Newport Harbor. There they saw its famous Round Tower, supposedly built by the Norsemen in 1000 A.D. This was one of Stoddard's long-anticipated historic features and he made some amusing comments about it and its authenticity.

Next day, convoyed by a fleet of cat-boats, the "Atlantis" headed past Seal Rocks and then toward the open sea once more and Martha's Vineyard. The wind died down temporarily and they were becalmed; the lull before the storm — hail this time. Then they were caught in an ugly chop and forced toward a reef. Running close-hauled and perilously close to the rocks they managed to cheat death by a narrow margin as a great swell bore them past on the bias and on to the safety of smoother water.

When the squall subsided the voyagers were able to use more sail and came alongside a schooner, whose captain invited them aboard; there they spent the night. During the next morning more dirty weather threatened so they put in to Edgartown Harbor. That night a perverse wind blew the "Atlantis" against the "Mary Ann McCann" with disastrous results. The prospect of heavy repairs forced Stoddard and Oblenis to put the canoe into Winter quarters, thus ending the first stage of the voyage.

The Second Stage of the Atlantis Cruise

Your devoted Bo'swain
R. B. Burchard.

R. B. Burchard

In 1884 Oblenis (the Professor) was unable to continue the voyage so Stoddard invited R. B. Burchard, secretary of the New York Canoe Club and editor of "The American Canoeist" to go with him. Although S. R. had never met him he had read his article on open water canoeing in the American Canoe Association magazine. He, Stoddard, was convinced that such an experienced companion would be both congenial and helpful. Therefore he contacted Burchard, who promptly accepted the invitation and described himself in the same letter. Then and there the photographer began to doubt the wisdom of his invitation, because the New Yorker pictured himself as a 250 pounder who doted on tobacco and strong onions (both of which Stoddard detested); he also snored and kicked in his sleep. However, since he had already gone this far, the man from Glens Falls decided not to renege on his offer but to cheerfully make the best of a bad bargain.

The first meeting of the two was very amusingly described by Stoddard. Instead of an immense, pipe-smoking ogre Burchard turned out to be a muscular stripling of twenty-five, nice-looking but with just a suspicion of the dude about him. Realizing that the prospective sailing companion did not recognize him and in order to get a better idea of the latter's real nature, S. R. pretended to be a salesman for faith cures, anti-fat remedies and a new type of life preserver. Burchard, taken in completely, treated Stoddard rather brusquely and tried to get rid of him. Finally Stoddard offered to sell him a deeply interesting and ridiculously cheap book, *The*

Adirondacks, written by himself. Thereupon Burchard claimed that he not only had the book but knew the author like a book. A long silence, then came the dawn of an idea in the young man's mind, followed by a heartfelt "I've - a - blamed - good - mind . . to - break - your - back!"

Burchard joined Stoddard at Woods Hole on July 4, 1883. His greeting consisted of the following torrent of words: "Hullo, owld man. Found you at last have I? Why in blazes didn't you leave word somewhere so't I wouldn't need to run all over town looking for you? That's the ship, is it? Great Guns, what a canoe! Wish my weepin' friends could see it, they'd feel easier. Where you stopping? Room for me? Left my trunk and bags over at the depot. Brought along a few things I thought we'd need — canned stuff that'll come in handy we get cast away on a desert island, and my binoculars to spy out pirates with, and a compass and a lot of charts - - . When will you be ready to start? And say how're you going to sleep nights — in the canoe or on shore? Got your life insured? I did. Had to pay double rates — said I kem under the head of extra-hazardous. Got some bully good cork life preservers and two more of the kind made of rubber that you put under your coat and blow up when you need them. What yer larfin at, you blawsted ijot? How long you been here? Had dinner yet? Bl'ieve I could eat a horse! How are you anyway? Say, you don't seem to say much. Holy Smoke! how hot it is! What's the matter? Got anything ketchin? Coz if you have I'm a goin'. Nothing but a fit I guess — chil'ns allers liable to have 'm."

For days afterward Stoddard's sides ached from laughing at his youthful companion's whimsical oddities, idiotic vaporings and outrageous absurdities. Crammed with the classics, his favorite quotations were of the "Good Ship Nancy Bell" order. Well-versed in the dead languages his renditions of the living ones would make people howl with apprehensive delight and the emeraldist Irishman in existence melt with envy for his country's brogue.

Quick in sympathy and generous beyond his reasonable means, he recklessly assumed loads that belonged to other backs. He wanted the Earth but if it didn't happen to be convenient to let him have it at a particular moment, he was rapturously content to sleep on the floor. Good fellowship surrounded him like a nimbus and he shed joy and personal belongings from New York to New Brunswick. He had serious objections to being hurried and habitually managed to arrive in a deliciously unconcerned sort of way just in time to swing aboard the rear platform of the last car just after the train had started. He didn't want anyone to mind him: they could go ahead if they couldn't wait. He'd buy a train of his own if necessary and come on when he got ready. All in all he was a highly entertaining and very competent person to have along on such a precarious journey, and the two venturesome canoeists were in for almost more tests of character and sailing skill than they could safely handle. Several times in fact they got generous and timely assists from both God and man.

Stoddard (at stern) and Burchard at Wood's Hole

Early on July 7th the "Atlantis" got under way and it took nine hours to beat their way against a strong headwind the twenty miles to Hyannis. The next morning, up at 4:40, they spent two hours covering the windy one mile from their starting place and had to rely on oars, a task which both disliked. Having been warned that owing to a recent storm it would be impossible to get through the surf at Chatham, they placed a touching confidence in both chart and compass and headed out for the southern tip of Monomoy Island. A freshening breeze turned into a full-grown gale during the later afternoon and then, as the darkness closed in, they saw the friendliest of sights — a lighthouse and the most beautiful strip of sand they had ever seen. Their only problem was to find the narrow passageway into the Powder Hole indicated on their supposedly reliable charts. After grounding repeatedly in the shoal water and being guided by a group of fishermen, they soon cast anchor in the quiet waters.

The lighthouse keeper, a Civil War veteran named Capt. Jones, and his family were very kind and interesting hosts to the canoeists. The Captain was a reservoir of anecdotes and coastal lore. He also gave them much sound advice about the rest of the voyage, particularly the route to Race Point, considered to be a fickle stretch of ocean. They then resumed their journey with the "Good-bye, may the Lord Preserve you!" of the brown old fisherman still lingering in their ears.

Toward night came the time when, as they had been warned, both wind and tide were against them and they found out why it was called Race Point. The velocity of the tide was so strong that they gained very little headway in spite of desperate maneuvering, but eventually they inched their way past the direful place and, with a favoring wind, passed Wood End Light, the haven of Provincetown, at 9 o'clock. This was their longest day and sail so far—an actual run of at least 86 miles although the chart showed but 62.

Sailing close-hauled into a strong wind it took from 1 P.M. until 11 P.M. for the "Atlantis" to navigate the less than 30 miles from Provincetown to Plymouth. The final three miles, when they had to negotiate the passage between the whistling buoy and the formidable Saquish Shoals in the darkness, contained a fair share of anxious moments....

The next morning the two intrepid travelers paid their respects to the shades of the Pilgrim dead on Burial Hill, visited Pilgrim Hall with its priceless collection of relics, saw the Rock and the other constant reminders of that dauntless company. Apparently even then the Pilgrim fathers were being exploited flagrantly and blatantly.

While Stoddard was settling some business on the dock, Buck (Burchard) went aboard the canoe to arrange things for their departure. What happened next was later overheard by S. R. "By gosh, boys," said the eyewitness to a crowd of his cronies, "You orter been down here a spell ago and seen the fun with them fellers that cum over the Bay last night. One of 'em stripped the cover off'n got some blame sort o' riggin' out and started to go by the mast on deck, 'kinder daisy-like you know, coz there was some gels alookin' on. Well, the canoe begun to tip and he hung onter the mast 'till ker-flop she went on her beam ends, spillin' out all the duffle and him with it, a kickin' and a-splutterin' in the water, an' the wimmen on the dock a squealin' like all Jim blazes. The uther feller, the tall, long-haired 'un, saw whut was happenin' 'n shoved off in a punt and picked up their gear and oars an a big watermellin and *then* towed the uther feller ashore. I'd jest like to be drowndin', *I* would, and have *that* feller come out to rescue me. Mebbe I ain't o'much account but I'm blamed if I don't b'lieve I'm as good as a watermellin any day!"

At 3 P.M. they left Plymouth and sailed into Scituate Harbor three hours later. There they saw the home of Samuel Woodworth, the author of the "Old Oaken Bucket," a man who did not always have the intense longing for pure water implied in the song. His granddaughter, a charming girl, understood the sentiment behind Stoddard's request for a drink from the famous well. But when the bucket appeared above the rim — it was a yawler (yellow) patent paper pail, not oak, and a mood was rudely shattered thereby.

Cohasset proved to be disappointing also because of their difficulty in finding quarters and an evening meal. After being turned away by the clerk at a private clubhouse and given an uncivil reception by a boozy public house proprietor, they finally got overnight accommodations in the home of a wary widow.

The next day, the twenty-first of the cruise, they passed Nantasket Beach, Boston, Nahant, Lynn, Marblehead and sailed into Gloucester Harbor in order to replenish their supplies of food and fuel for the ingenious stove. They spent that night aboard the canoe. After a sumptuous breakfast of soup, bacon, omelet, griddlecakes and coffee the voyage was resumed. Past Newburyport, Hampton Harbor and the Isle of Shoals they sailed as the wind accelerated in velocity and bore them away from the long swells and into the chop toward shore. Since the canoe's length as compared with beam was her weakness, they were in deep trouble. A double flood filled the craft, and, as they balanced it as best they could, a huge wave rendered the rudder useless (out of water). Over went the "Atlantis," mast and sail flat upon the water; the two men kicking themselves loose from the entangling canvas.

Humiliated and surprised because they had thought the little boat capable of living through almost any gale, Stoddard and Burchard worked themselves free from the cover. They righted the canoe with great difficulty. Waterlogged clothing hampered their efforts to unship the mast, however, and over they went again — and the treadmill routine had to be resumed. Finally Stoddard secured his knife, cut away the cordage and threw the wreckage overboard; next they jettisoned most of their cargo and bailed out as much of the water as possible in view of the fact that more kept pouring in.

They were in a serious predicament and gradually realized its full nature. "We reasoned that the strong wind would drive us into the harbor, or at worst, on the shore, in which case we must stick to the canoe until she struck and then take our chances of getting through the surf with as few bruises as possible. I did not then know that our fight was not against the water only but against numbness which would take away all power of resistance and motion until its victim becomes as a frozen clod except for the fearfully alert brain. We then began to realize something of this silent force when the conviction came at last that we could do practically nothing to influence our course. We kept on paddling, however, to combat as far as possible the chill that was taking possession of us. It was an element that had not entered my calculations. Matters were beginning to look decidedly unpleasant.

"How long can you stand this?" I asked.

"Not very long — legs beginning to cramp now," was the reply.

"Well, pull with all your might, old man, and keep your blood moving."

"Yes," with mournful disgust, "and use up all your strength in doing it!"

"This view of the matter had not occurred to me. The question was one that evidently had two sides to it. So we continued to paddle in a desultory way until Buck shouted, "Hurrah! Help's coming!'

"Over my shoulder as we rose on the waves I saw a schooner with sails winged out driving directly at us. Our troubles were forgotten in the excitement of the moment. Did they see us? If not they certainly could not miss us as they came nearer. After a time she changed her course to pass us on the left about an eighth of a mile away.

"She's bearing off to round up into the wind and pick us up," Buck explained. We waited patiently to see her come about — but when abreast of us she showed no motion, either of men or of sails to indicate her intention of doing anything of the kind.

"They don't see us! Yell! Yell like Hell!!!'

"We shouted ourselves weak but the schooner continued on her course and those on board gave no sign that they understood our plight except that a knot of men gathered at the rail made incomprehensible motions as if hurrahing at us."

'They think we're doing this for fun," he said, 'They're leaving us without even trying to see whether we need help or not!' I am afraid that this carefully-reared son of a D.D. misquoted scriptural phrases in a way not taught him by his reverend father. His remarks seemed very appropriate."

Suddenly they noticed that the men on the schooner were signaling them to look to windward. They did and at first saw only a dreary expanse of angry waters breaking toward them. Then, poised on the top of a huge wave, they saw it plainly — a dory. Next came the long wait while the rescue boat made its way toward them at what seemed to be a snail's pace.

"We were getting terribly cold, shaking with an exhausting ague that would not give us a second's rest. Our teeth were chattering like castanets, our muscles drawn to their utmost tension and straining fiercely against each other in a vain endeavor to be still. A deathly chill clung around the laboring heart and our bodies felt as though sheeted in ice.

"The boat neared us and developed into a much larger one than I had at first supposed, and it was being handled with infinite skill by the burly man at the oars.

'Oh, hurry up, can't you?' called Buck.

'Don't get excited now," said the man in a matter-of-fact tone as he warily sized up the situation. 'Things'll all come around in time if you don't hurry.'

'Now, captain,' said the man reassuringly, 'the first smooth water that comes, I'm goin' to lay up alongside you. Do you think you are able to keep the boats from foulin?'

"Could I? Why didn't he ask me something hard?"

'Don't you forget now,' he added, 'for if I come down on you just once that craft o'your's is a goner as sure as there's a Lord above. Mind another thing too': don't either o'you try to get in her 'til I give the word. I've got no mind to have my boat go over in this sea. Now ready all and when I bring them together, look out — and be lively when I tell you!'

"As the next wave passed, the stranger dexterously laid his boat alongside the "Atlantis" and the two men, getting hold of Burchard's collar, helped that willing gentleman over the rail in short order."

'Thanks awfully — no need of an introduction. Don't mind my shine!' were the words of the irrepressible as he landed in the bottom of the dory.

"When I had the rail of the stranger under my hands, I could hardly resist the inclination to leave the uncertain support of the canoe, now appearing so utterly unworthy of confidence. In my excitement I stood up on her slippery deck and, when I saw that friendly hands had grasped my companion, I took no thought as to the manner of going but went. Giving a final push that would separate the two, and with a scrambling leap, I landed in a heap among the cordage of the larger craft."

Checking his watch, which had stopped at 1:58 P.M., Stoddard found that they had been in the icy water more than an hour and a half. The schooner attempted to tow the waterlogged "Atlantis" but, since it yawed wildly, it was abandoned. The two bedraggled men were helped aboard the "Bellow", hustled down into the cabin, where Buck was given warm clothes, a generous glass of Jamaica ginger and occupancy of the Captain's bunk.

Stoddard managed to get out of his clinging clothes almost without assistance and when faced with the alternatives of letting his clothes dry on him or changing into dry duds but thereby risking a cold, had the decision made for him. The Captain stripped off his own flannel shirt and

104

Portsmouth Harbor — Pilot Aimee's House

made the shivering man don it.

That day they found out that their rescuer was Capt. G. D. Amee, whose home was at Kittery Point inside the entrance to Portsmouth Harbor. By keeping close tabs on the shipping news he knew when vessels bound for Portsmouth were due to arrive and watched for them. On the day of the rescue a bright-eyed boy named Vaney Rand had first seen them in the water but, since the canoe itself didn't show up in the binoculars, had been told that it was just his fancy. The boy, however, kept insisting and the men finally confirmed the discovery and started the rescue operation.

Burchard and Stoddard stayed with the Amees for several days during which the Captain and his "little woman" took pardonable pride in exhibiting the canoeists. "We had to be shipwrecked and drowned and discovered and yanked over into the "Gracie" again and again with various emendations, additions and corrections; strongly italicized, copiously capitalized and richly illustrated; with footnotes by the authors and sworn affidavits regarding the circulation by the publishers."

The "Atlantis" was re-discovered almost uninjured when she stranded on a sandy beach; her finder was made reasonably happy by a substantial reward. Three or four rubber bags, oars and paddles also had come ashore. Photographic negatives of the "Old Oaken Bucket" were still good and the books and charts, though watersoaked were not entirely ruined.

A valuable camera which had been stowed away in a rubber bag was scarcely wet at all. The jettisoned sails were never recovered.

Three days later, decked out in a new suit of sails, the "Atlantis," to the accompaniment of deafening cheers, sailed away again. "We would have been just as well satisfied if they hadn't been so enthusiastic. We had looked for tears."

Pointing outward, the twenty-third day of the cruise began as they passed under the guns of the North Atlantic Squadron anchored there, rounded inside Whale's-back and hugged the eastward shore for most of the morning before mustering the necessary confidence to venture farther out.

At 5:30 they rounded into Biddeford Pool, where they found that a rumor had preceded them that the voyage had been abandoned. They were congratulated and forced to listen to comforting discussions as to their chances of continuing safely or getting drowned; a majority of the advisors seemed to believe that the latter alternative would be the legitimate result if they persisted with their plan.

The next morning being foggy they delayed their departure until tired of the inactivity and then steered a compass course for Cape Elizabeth. Later, as the fog lifted, they passed Old Orchard Beach, then crept up to Cape Elizabeth and around Portland Head into that harbor. That night the canoe found welcome at the Union Boat House and the voyagers at the Preble House. There also ended the second phase of the eventful cruise of the "Atlantis."

Chapter 9

The Cruise of the Atlantis
Third Phase of the Voyage

On the third leg of the nearly 2,000 mile odyssey of the "Atlantis" Stoddard had still another companion with whom to share the pleasures and perils. This man, Capt. G. D. Amee, was the husky Downeaster who had snatched the photographer and his friend Burchard from the frigid waters off Portsmouth. A licensed pilot he had shown considerable interest in the voyage and had even said that he wouldn't mind sailing in her himself if ever he got the opportunity. That opportunity arose when Burchard was unable to rejoin S. R. and Amee promptly accepted the offer. By doing so he showed a willingness to take chances which most seasoned seafarers had considered to be far too unfavorable, even though they willingly took such gambles daily in their dories.

"Capt. Amee made an agreeable boatmate; he was original, unconventional, and he thought for himself. He was not so old as to be beyond the reach of a joke, nor so young as to suppose he knew everything. He knew the thoroughfares where the larger vessels went up and down like a well-thumbed book, but I now found that he knew no more of the inner ways where the "Atlantis" was to go than I did, and all my knowledge of the coast came only from the chart. I was glad of that too for it would have taken half the interest away to have had someone always telling what was coming next. In some ways he was invaluable: he gave me more points about handling small craft in rough water than I had ever learned before and, most remarkable of all, he rather enjoyed rowing. The only bad thing about him was a habit he had of ignoring the dishes after our occasional noonday meal."

Following a debate over the advisability of setting out in a thick fog, a discussion which was used by Amee to test Stoddard's seamanship and general judgment, the pilot summed it up in this way: "All right, you're the doctor and will be the captain too if you go through there with your eyes shut. I want either an open course or a chance to see my way when I'm running a ship. You'll have neither today when you get away from the mainland — but I'm with you if you say so." "So we went. Incidentally as far as being captain was concerned I had no objections; in fact such had been my intention all the time."

The little craft threaded its way slowly through the fog, guided by compass, chart, marker buoys and the warning sound of surf on dangerous reefs. Toward evening they made Bailey's Island, where they were put up for the night by a garrulous, generous old seaman and his eccentric mother, who shattered the nocturnal silence with her loud and fervent prayers.

"Models of vessels full-rigged and ready for the sea cluttered the house. Pictures of ships adorned the walls, along with those of Jack in immaculate collar and streamered hat and of Jack's sweetheart with corkscrew curls and pensive air and the most improbable of waists. Pictures of the sailor's goodbye and of his joyous return to his numerous and well-laundered family. And yet another likeness, one found in many a New England home, of the greenest of weeping willows hanging over the whitest of marble slabs and on the white surface — a written name and an inscription.

"But men must work and women must weep and the same old story is told in hundreds of homes along the coast every year. The number that lie out on the treeless hill is greater by far than the living, and on the poor headstones the women's names outnumber, two to one, the men's. Mothers give up their sons and wives their husbands, with fears that seemed dulled by familiarity with danger, knowing that many will be called yet hoping always that theirs will not be the one chosen. And the fisheries prosper and the staple food of the poor is cheap, for the lives that it is bought with have no redemption value in the commercial world."

The youngest son of the family, a splendid, modest, rather slow-moving man, was impatiently biding his time and counting the days before he too could break the home ties. In the meantime he was satisfying his longing for action and earning a living by being the spearman of a swordfishing schooner, a job that called for the coolest head, the surest hand and the strongest arm because a thousand-pounder is not uncommon among that species.

Said he without a trace of boasting, "I have had 'leven swords struck at one time and barrels floating about like buoys over a lobster ground and we saved every one of them. Swords seem logy-like when they're swimmin' around but when they're struck if they're not hurt purty bad — only enough to make them mad — then look out! They drive right for you savage as anything and if they hit you you'll think lightnin' struck you. They'll shiver a small boat all to flinters and will drive their swords right through the bottom of a ship sometimes as though it was nothin' but paper. They leave a piece of it there, usually with the point stickin' through the plankin' inside. I ironed one once that had his sword broken off more than half way up, and I know of a schooner that had one drove right through the keel and it was an oak keel at that. They just sawed the sword off smooth on each side and left it there."

The charge of a night's lodging and three meals each was reckoned by their hostess to be a total of twenty-five cents. They paid a dollar and Stoddard made this revealing and heartfelt remark: "I want to go there again sometime before some whited syndicate descends on the place and puts up a big, glaring, gong-haunted caravansary, to change the native, sweet simplicity into brazen cash and turn loose on a long-suffering public that devil-fish which fattens in the baleful shadow of the big hotel and worms its clammy, many-suckered tentacles into his victim's innermost pocket under the delusive guise of attentive service!"

The following day they had reached the mouth of the Kennebec River before becoming fog-bound again near Sequin Island. There they encountered some particularly rough going similar to that of the memorable day off Portsmouth. However, Pilot Amee's superior seamanship and Stoddard's navigational ability took them through safely to Cape Newagen and the end of the twenty-sixth day of the venture.

Capt. Gray, their host, was the pioneer and the great man of the hamlet. He represented in a small way both the teeming wealth of ocean and the fostering industries of land. From him they learned much about codfishing and processing for the market. Although Amee displayed a great liking for the oil — licked it off his thumb as Northern New Yorkers would maple syrup — Stoddard's recollections of boyhood registered an internal protest against the stuff.

The twenty-seventh day opened with the usual fog blanket shrouding all objects. The pilot's manner of asking for orders caused Stoddard to revise his plans and drew the following reaction from the former:

"How'd you expect to get where you want to go in this fog?"

"Chart and compass."

"How you going to figger on the tide among the islands?"

"Tide tables and guessing."

"How about the rocks and shoal?"

"Ears — musical ears."

"Well, you've got the ears all right — no question about *that*."

Soon afterward they had picked their way through the fleet of fishing boats and out to sea. When Stoddard's rudder-work brought them right on time at a designated lighthouse, Amee dropped his oars, or as nearly so as a sailor can, and his lower jaw at the same time and looked quickly around. "By the Lord Harry there she is!" he said: then he laughed uneasily to cover his obvious anxiety. From that point on the pilot seldom questioned the captain's judgment and navigating knack.

Toward noon Pemaquid Point was passed. Then toward sunset the mouth of the Weskiag River ("Skeg") and South Thomaston. Next morning they made the run to Owl's Head, then past Rockland, Penobscot Bay and the "Thoroughfare" between the Fox Islands, past North Haven and anchorage and a hearty welcome from a Capt. Young and his family, who were lobster fishermen.

The next afternoon saw them through the Deer Islands, where the previously uneventful leg was enlivened by their nearly smashing in the keel of the canoe on a submerged rock. They spent that night at Stinson's Neck.

The thirtieth day was a rainy, dreary one with a contrary wind but they followed a course which took them through Bartlett's Narrows and Western Bay to Mt. Desert Island, where a pleasure party on a six-ton yacht which had ridden out the storm in the harbor refused to believe that the two had come from Stinson's Neck that morning in a canoe.

The final day of the third stage of the cruise was ushered in by Amee's prediction of an impending gale from the northeast and the warning that the sooner they cast off the better. Although there were no indications of such a storm at that time, it materialized soon enough and they made a lively two-hour trip down the northeast shore of the island to Bar Harbor. There the two parted — Amee for his home by the afternoon boat, while Stoddard remained for a mild indulgence in the dissipations of that famous resort.

The highlight of his brief sojourn there was the cog-railroad trip to the top of Green Mountain, fifteen hundred feet above the Harbor. A recent fire had destroyed the old hotel and Stoddard was the first lodger in the section of the new one just begun. He was awakened during the night by shrill voices of girls singing and the frenzied pounding of feet all keeping time. It was the workmen and their girls having a social dance in the room below.

"It was glorious up there! Nature had done much for the place. The view was superb, the air wonderful, the sunset most beautiful, the sunrise glorious and the great star-studded concave, stooping downward at night, made heaven itself seem near.

"And the landlord put it all in the bill!"

The Fourth Leg of the Cruise

The fourth stage of the voyage of the gallant little "Atlantis" started at Bar Harbor on August 23, 1886 with R. B. Burchard as the other member of the crew. Buck had a new song for every year and that year it was "White Wings." With Stoddard supplying the "plink plink" accompaniment they made most striking music together. "I think he was one of the most independent singers I ever listened to, and as for expression — I have often even on the warmest of days felt that creepy sensation, the involuntary tribute to genius, running up and down my spine just listening to him. Sometimes when he became fired with the inexpressible harmony of a noble theme, he would drop into the cavernous depths of his de profundis and his thrilling tones would become indescribable. It made me think somehow of a bumblebee under a tin pan.

110

Mt. Desert Island, Green Mtn. R.R.

Bar Harbor, Mt. Desert, Me.

"We each sang solos at times and on such occasions the other was expected to drop in on the chorus for all he was worth. I often, by request and in my modest way, favored him with one of my favorites, one quite appropriate for a canoe cruise. The first line was 'Oh if a storm should rouse the deep, what matter? What matter? I will ride and sleep.' Usually this made a great impression on him and he would sing it with vigor even in the public streets. Once in the middle of the night he came close to creating a panic in the public house where we were stopping by howling out the line in frenzied fervor."

From Bar Harbor, where they had spent three days in riotous pleasure by being entertained by other nautical friends who offered sage advice, they made the 25 miles to Bois Bubert ("Bo-Bear") Island, where they spent the night with a farmer-fisherman. Equipped with a new set of sails but with the same reefing gear as used in 1883, they reached Jonesport, where a heavy fog cut short that day's journey and gave them time to see a sardine cannery in operation.

On the thirty-third day they passed Mark Island, the most easterly point laid down on their chart, with an impending storm muttering away in the distance. A few hours later they reached Libby Island and its lighthouse, where more than twenty vessels had been known to have foundered. All that afternoon they had been sailing through drifting lath and lumber which had formed the cargo of a schooner which had been wrecked only two days before, and another that had been rammed by a larger craft had drifted ashore just the night before, the crew barely escaping with their lives.

Burchard was greatly interested that night in the topic of wrecked ships and required a vast amount of personal information from the lighthouse keeper's pretty daughter with whom he delved into the musty records, oblivious to passing time until finally Stoddard felt obliged to drag him away for the night.

With the sun an hour high the next day, the thirty-fourth of the voyage, they rounded the red and yellow cliff of West Quoddy Head, the easternmost tip of Maine and of the United States and, borne by the swift tide, they landed at Eastport just at nightfall.

By noon the next day they had reached Her Majesty's Lighthouse at Head Harbor on the Bay of Fundy. The Nova Scotia peninsula protected them from the direct force of the great ocean waves so from that time on they had little difficulty in landing at any point. Their main obstacles were to be the sudden storms and fogs and more menacing — the irresistible power of the tides which had carried many boats out to sea never to be heard from again. At Seely Cove, a desolate spot, they finally found lodging for the night with a "foin old Irish gintleman" and his sons. They slept on the floor of the cabin using their own bedrolls.

The following day they followed the coast for some distance before attempting the eight miles of open water to Point Lepreau. Reduced sail and a bottle of oil were essentials in combatting the high winds and waves. Passing Lepreau they had even harder going in order to reach the coastline. At Split Rock a schooner lay keeled over, high and dry. Prime factors involved — projecting point, high tide, fog and a drunken captain.

"The coast here is magnificent. Added to the grand outline of cliff and rugged hill is the charm of varied color. Here are rocks black as coal, red as blood, yellow as sulphur, while the foliage ranges from darkest olive to the most delicate emerald. The cliffs rise straight up from the water with scarcely a break in the walls. They are the Palisades run wild, a nightmare formation twisted into fantastic shapes and weird, hideous forms. Here a Titanic horse rises, with dripping flanks and turns his head landward to feed upon the tree tops; there the sea serpent climbs and coils himself among the rocks; nearby, a death's head with ghastly, grinning teeth and empty eyesockets stares out across the Bay."

Here also they got an example of the force of the tide: The wind was strong enough and they moved through the water at a fair rate. But the tide came from exactly the point they were trying to reach, so they spent fully an hour sailing steadily yet all the while keeping directly opposite a certain cleft in the rocks, gaining nothing, barely holding their own. Finally they managed by desperate rowing to reach the muddy flats of the Pisaringo and the welcome land. Nine people refused them accommodations before the tenth let them sleep in a big feather bed — on the floor of the best room.

Being turned down so often was a new experience for them because heretofore they had usually had little difficulty. But here on the Bay of Fundy there seemed to be invisible bars put up at every door against them.

Next morning with a light following wind they sailed into the harbor of St. John. They moored the "Atlantis" beside a high dock and climbing up sought some necessary information. Later, when the tide came in it lifted the little craft and, with the aid of sundry helpful citizens, cranes and tackle they took her out of the water and placed her in the Storehouse, there to await final shipment home. This act ended the fourth phase of the Cruise of the canoe "Atlantis."

The Fifth and Final Phase of the Cruise of the "Atlantis"

On Wednesday, August 4, 1887 the "Atlantis," Stoddard and Burchard sailed away from St. John. Buck's new song was "Adieu, Adieu, Adieu" — with variations, mostly in the music not in the words. To the southeast stretched the faint blue line of Nova Scotia. Just before their departure they had been told that "whenever you can see Nova Scotia from St. John, get ready for a storm."

The fishermen at Pisaringo had told them about the remarkable tides they had to contend with and that they always went in couples with a net stretched between them. They never attempted to buck the tide except for short distances. Generally they just drifted with it. These details impressed the Americans but did not deter them. The lack of deep water harbors also constituted a potent hazard, the only two being at Maitland and Horton. An account of an encounter with "The Bore" also influenced their thinking.

"We heered it a bit before it cum a-rollin' and a-roarin' and a 'splashin' an' a-boomin'; nigher'n nighern'n, louder'n louder every minute and it made me feel streaked all over I tell you. But we couldn't do nothin' but jest wait. Then we see it a'comin' through the dark like a big bank 'shin'. It seemed to be jest a-rollin' over'n over, fairly a-spinnin' as it cum, an' whar it broke over in front, it 'peared to flash like sheet-lightnin' an' the wind seemed to be all sucked away f'm us fur a minit . . . Then it cum like a hurrycane an' struck us 'bout the same time as the bore did an' Lord! fur as much as a minit I thought sartin we'd be stove, or flung up on our beam-ends, fur it struck us broadside and jest histed us right off'n the bottom — parted the chain like a piece of pack-thread an' left the anchor out thar in the mud.

"The next wave that cum wan't as big as the fust 'un, and the next wuz littler yet but it sot us adrift. I won't pertend to say how big that *fust* one was. I don't think you'd b'lieve me, but one thing I *will* say: we draw'd two fathom — twelve feet of water — an when that *third* wave got under us — we floated! You don't git sech big ones as them of'n, but I guess most any of 'em would be 'bout's much az you'd wanta tackle."

Such anecdotes and warnings made them understandably thoughtful so they had been duly impressed, especially so when they knew that this last leg of the trip would be through wider convolutions than they had previously experienced. Having passed forbidding Cape Spencer and approaching McCoy Head, they met the returning tide. They entered the disturbed area and became its plaything as recollections of the ordeal off Portsmouth came flooding back. They traversed that stretch without incident, however, and were a short time later helped ashore by some men building a ship in a cove. The builder, William Wallace, gave them a fascinating explanation of the techniques of shipbuilding and its history in those waters, and also some sound advice concerning the next portion of the trip. At Salmon River, a lumber port, they ended the thirty-ninth day at the home of Squire Foster.

On the fortieth day they started out for grim Cape Chignecto, were nearly caught in heavy tide rips en route, but fortunately reached Chicken Neck, as Buck called it, in the proverbial nick of time. From there they could see Cape D'Or and its lighthouse, but the six miles which separated them from Advocate Village, where they expected to pass the night, were trying ones, so they went ashore at the lighthouse and there spent the night in the "Atlantis."

In the morning they sailed across the bay to Advocate Village and the looked-for breakfast — eggs, two or three varieties of bread, cold biscuit, two kinds of pie, seed-cakes and tea. Then, guided by a native, they made their way through a mighty crooked channel to a broad swift river which led them to the sea. Several hours later they rounded Cape Spencer and headed toward Cape Split, nine foggy miles away and the home of more heavy tide rips. Since conditions began to look unfavorable they compromised and put into Port Greville for the night.

Warned against the deceits practiced by the waters off Blumidon (Blow-me-down) mountain, they were prepared for the struggle against the fierce west wind which struck them. They made it safely past this landmark and found pleasant quarters in a farmhouse, where they were surprised to learn that the graceful daughter, who would have made an ideal Evangeline, had never heard of Longfellow's tragic heroine. With characteristic gallantry Burchard volunteered to send her a copy of the poem as soon as he got back to New York.

On the forty-third day the canoeists, from the safety of land, saw tides which rose more than eighty feet and filled the Basin of Minas brimful. After a long wait they were able to sail up the Horton River to the landing place of ancient Grand Pre, home of Evangeline. "Of the ancient village of Grand Pre little remains save tradition. Lines of old dykes, built by the Acadians before their dispersal by the British in 1755, remain along with the stones of cellars and an old well, from which water is still taken. The supposed site of the old church is also pointed out, and rows of huge willows are said to mark the course of ancient streets. And this is all.

"Grand Pre has its little railroad station, built in deference to the past and to supply a foreign demand rather than a local need. Here come flocks of callow youth of all ages — mostly from 'the States' — with Longfellow in their shawlstraps and Evangeline at their tongues' end; spoony young men and romantic maidens full of sentiment and with tears on tap they swarm out of the train when it stops, gathering handfuls of grass and weeds for mementoes, clutching wildly at the struggling daisies; raiding the willows; splintering the fences and bearing away great gobs of mud from the swales where the cattails grow.

"They even secured a secondhand coffin (once said to have been occupied by one of the Acadian peasants ever since his friends had deserted him by order of the British long ago) and held it on exhibition in the station waiting-room here; an object of mournful inspection until sliver by sliver, it melted away before the all-devouring, relic-hunting, Yankee jackknife. We had to be content with willow, however, because when we arrived the railroad people were all out of coffins."

Burchard hit exactly the right note one day as they were strolling along to the dactylic-hexameter gait. Repeating the opening lines of the poem he stopped suddenly and exclaimed, "Commodore, it's a big sell! There haint no forest primeval; there haint no deep-voiced neighboring ocean and there haint a durned whispering pine or a hemlock within forty miles of here — les' go'n look for the bore." This revelation ended the forty-fourth day.

"Every day but one of the cruise since leaving St. John had its exciting hours and moments when there appeared to be good reason for care. I doubt if we could have sailed out of the Bay of Fundy had we started from its head with only the experience that was ours when we left New York. But working gradually toward the more difficult part of the course we acquired a confidence and a certain skill that could be gained only by actual experiences and without which we could not have gone successfully through the later stages of the cruise. There in the region of high tides, difficulties multiplied due mainly to rapid and violent atmospheric disturbances."

On the forty-fifth day they left Tennycape Harbor bound first for Maitland, twenty-three miles away, but adverse conditions cut their sailing to only three hours. Capt. McDougal, ship-builder, mill-owner and patron of that section, put them up for the night.

The next morning they started early but immediately ran into trouble in full view of the people who had entertained them the night before and who had evidently acquired a high opinion of their seamanship. The peak halyard broke and let the mainsail come thrashing down. Fast work by Buck with his knife gave them a leg-of-mutton sail which got them out of their embarrassment and out with the flood tide. To compound their predicament Burchard next discovered that they had left the anchor at Tennycape. Constant tacking over a big mudbank finally solved that problem and they were now approaching the narrow upper end of the Bay. When they reached shore two natives, who had been watching them, caught the painter and made it fast to a tree.

"Thanks — nice morning," said Buck.

"Well, if that ain't the fooniest riggin' I ever seed in shape ov a bo-at,' said one of the two in open-mouthed wonder.

"We wuz a watchin' yous ever since you cum in sight," said the other.

"An't looked so awful foony, scootin' along in the bottom of the creek — couldn't see much only yer heads on the sail!"

"Do you ever see anything of the "Bore" up this way?" inquired Buck.

"Youp. See'm mos' every day," was the reply.

"How big is it?"

"Oh, guess two, three foot — mebby more; I've seed 'em 'ere much as six feet.

"Commodore," said Buck with enthusiasm, "we've druv him into his hole! Let's after!"

Instead, they waited until the channel had filled and then sailed the mile and a half to Truro; there at the head of navigation they ran the slender prow of the "Atlantis" onto the muddy shore and her long journey was ended.

End of the Cruise of the Atlantis

117

"Old man," said Buck, putting out his hand as he stepped with one foot on the canoe and the other resting on land until I had likewise a foot on each, "shake, this is for all time remember."

"Dear boy! There was the faintest trace of a tremble in his voice as he spoke and I suspect that he was really in earnest — for the moment at least.

"And the 'Atlantis'?"

"The red water ebbed away out toward the distant ocean and left her lying there, the helpless object of our care. But her work was done — and well done. She had accomplished that for which she had been created."*

---

*In the appendix is a St. John's *Globe* account of the voyage of the doughty little "Atlantis" and her dauntless crew.

Chapter 10

The Alaska Interlude

On the night of July 17, 1892 S. R. Stoddard, accompanied by R. B. Burchard of New York, left Glens Falls by train for Montreal, the starting point for their long-planned trip to Alaska. Burchard, a secretary of the American Canoe Association, had previously shared with Stoddard the excitement and hazards of the cruise to the Bay of Fundy via the New England coastline in the canoe "Atlantis." Both looked forward to another interesting trip together, a journey which would also provide the photographer with the necessary material for another lecture program. This was the first of five long trips which Stoddard made during the five-year period which followed.

Late the next afternoon they boarded a Canadian Pacific train for the six-day transcontinental trip to Tacoma, Washington. The first day out brought little of interest to them because that part of Canada is relatively monotonous. The second day's ride, along the wild rugged north shore of Lake Superior, provided far more scenic appeal. On the third day they crossed endless miles of Manitoba's grain belt, where golden wheatfields stretched in every direction to the distant horizon.

At Winnipeg, the capital of the prairie province, they saw a few imposing buildings but for the most part that home for 30,000 people had little that interested the travelers. It was still growing rapidly and showed all its growing pains. At Regina they got their first glimpse of the Indians, whose tepees dotted the plains. The red men and their squaws gathered around the station, the bucks in their gaudy blankets and feathers and their fat wives loaded with beadwork and articles for sale.

When Stoddard unlimbered his camera, they seemed to regard it with a superstitious awe that nearly panicked them. Singling out one group of three braves he tried to get them to stay together long enough to snap the shutter, but they scattered like rabbits — two scurried behind the station while the third scrambled under a nearby freight car. The squaws hastily covered their faces with their blankets and pulled the papooses under with them.

Regina was the headquarters for the Mounted Police of which there were about a thousand posted along the line from Manitoba to the Rockies. They patrolled constantly to keep both Indians and whites under control and to prevent cattle rustling.

At Calgary, sixty miles east of the mountains, the two Americans spent their most interesting day of the trip up to that point. By invitation of a Mr. Costigan, the Queen's Prosecutor for that district, they visited an Indian reservation ten miles to the south. There they saw savages in all their ancient filth if not wildness. Save for a breechcloth their only necessary covering seemed to be a universal crust of dirt. Apparently all their clothing was saved for special occasions or cold weather.

These were the Sarcees, reputed to be the wickedest as well as the lowest of the natives of the West. They lived in squalor under the almost absolute control of the government agent, who doled out to them what they needed for survival. They lived in tepees with the usual smokehole in the top. As was true of the other tribes the squaws did all the heavy work.

The Sarcees customarily buried — if it can be called that — their dead in the tops of trees or occasionally, as did some of the mountain tribes, left them under blankets in an abandoned tepee. The chiefs often had several wives.

Members of this tribe made a big show of violent objections to having their pictures taken so Stoddard had to either bribe them or trip the shutter stealthily. Most of the Indians, however, soon succumbed to the offer of money for posing. The scale ranged from fifty cents for the common brave up to five dollars, the princely sum extorted by the surly chief Bullhead.

From there the travelers got their first view of the Rockies looming up on the skyline like a long, impenetrable wall. Back aboard the train and on to Banff Hot Spa, a mountain resort much like the Yellowstone Park. A little farther west and the train crossed the Continental Divide over the route which had been completed in 1867, twenty-seven years previously. The scenery was of course spectacular: the black canyons, rushing rivers, high-pinnacled snowsheds, and vast snowfields of the Selkirks; the myriad lakes and dense growths of evergreens below the timberline — all these were very impressive to men used to the tamer attractions of the older Adirondacks.

Then came the descent into the valley between the Rockies and the Selkirk Range, along the Columbia and across it to the Fraser, which they followed southward through British Columbia and on to the Pacific coast of Washington State.

Stoddard's strongest impression of the long trip across Canada was the notable lack of the hustling quality characteristic of many of the American frontier settlements. The railroad employees in particular didn't seem to care whether the trains ran on time or not. Nearly all the people

Sarcee Squaws

Sarcee Indian family

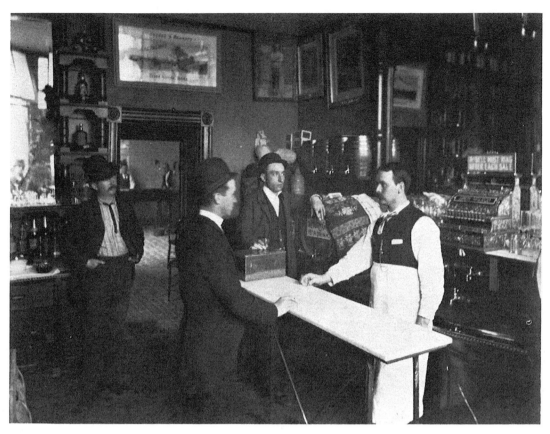

A Bar room, Pacific Coast

Totem poles of Chief Shacks

failed to show the drive and enterprise of the settlers in Seattle and Tacoma.

Port Townsend, Washington was an exception because that once-prosperous town was, in 1892, fast dropping into decay. Very few signs of vitality were discernible; gambling seemed to be the principal interest of the residents.

On July 27th the two companions sailed from the declining seaport aboard the "City of Topeka" bound for Alaska via the Inside Passage, on a journey of nearly a thousand miles. Only occasionally did the boat feel the rollers from the Pacific, but when that happened many of the sixty passengers suddenly lost interest in eating. Stoddard was one of only four who never missed the five meals provided on shipboard.

The magnificent scenery of the Passage made its full impact on the photographer, who took pictures all along the route to St. Mary's Island in southern Alaska, their first port of call. After a brief stop there the steamer put in at Metlakahtla, near Ketchikan, where a Mr. Duncan, an English missionary, was in control as the result of a grant from the United States. He had set up a semi-religious community without any clearly-defined creed. About 250 natives worked at the salmon cannery under the supervision of five white men, assistants of Duncan.

The natives had very primitive ideas of virtue: they believed it perfectly proper to steal from the whites but among themselves were reasonably honest. Smuggling was carried on extensively, especially in whiskey. This represented a curious paradox: although the U.S. government prohibited the sale of liquor in Alaska, licenses were granted to all applicants.

Fort Wrangell, the next place visited, was extremely interesting to the travelers. The Stickeen Indians who lived nearby furnished fascinating material for many pictures. The painted totem poles, each bearing various images to designate tribe or clan, had receptacles in their bases for the ashes of the dead. Three old women, who having outlived their usefulness had been driven away[1] by their children, evoked special concern. To Stoddard this treatment of the aged exemplified the worst kind of cruelty but was, of course, a tribal custom to which the victims never rebelled. The survival of the fittest has always been cruel but nevertheless imperative among people for whom mere existence has always been precarious.

The photographer heard of an aged squaw, said to be over ninety and the widow of a famous chief. Getting an interpreter they arrived at her hut at midnight. There they found her in the characteristic pose — knees drawn up under her chin and hands clasped over her feet. The flash picture which S. R. made of this matriarch of the tribe was undoubtedly among the most memorable of all those he took on the trip.

---

1.   Stoddard was obviously in error here because traditionally the older men and women voluntarily went off to die in order that the abler, younger members of the tribe might have a better chance to survive.

The Alaskan Indians lacked the splendid physique of the Plains Indians and looked more like Esquimaux. They had big heads, heavy bodies and diminutive legs. The latter characteristic was explained by their traveling so much in canoes and represents a type of atrophy. Every male Indian seemed to have a dugout, which was as necessary to him as the horse was to the red men of the Plains. These craft were made of white or yellow cedar and presented nearly perfect lines from a shipbuilder's viewpoint.

From Fort Wrangell the next place on the "Topeka's" itinerary was Juneau, the largest town in Alaska, whose main attraction was the placer mining. Neighboring Douglas Island had the world's largest and most productive ore processing plant, valued at nearly twice the sum paid to Russia — $7,200,000 — for Alaska in 1867, only twenty-five years before.

Sitka, then capital and residence of the governor, was the next town visited. An ancient Russian settlement with many traces of the past remaining, including Baranof's cattle, it had much appeal. Its greatest feature was the Graeco-Russian orthodox church with its treasures of religious art, one of them supposedly a lost Raphael Madonna. The treatment of the paintings was unusual in that every portion except the faces of the figures was covered with hammered silver. The two Americans attended the farewell service for Bishop Nicholas, the head of the American branch and in charge of eleven churches in his diocese, eight of which were in Alaska.

Glacier Bay with its eleven tidal glaciers, among them the vast (800 square miles) Muir iceflow, was probably the highlight of the journey. While it moves at the rate of seven feet every twenty-four hours it nevertheless, like Niagara, has a crest that is constantly receding and is now several miles farther inland from where it was when Vancouver discovered it 100 years before. While the ship's passengers were watching it in awe, a huge mass broke off the two hundred-foot face of the glacier and fell slowly and majestically into the depths below. On the run to Chilkat they saw more than forty during the intervening seventy-five miles.

Pyramid Harbor, only thirty miles from the mouth of the Yukon River and only 450 miles from the Arctic Circle, was the northernmost point of the voyage. There, in June, the sun rose at 3 a.m. and set at 11 p.m., when there was still light enough for Stoddard to read on deck. The polar star was so far overhead that it tired his neck to look at it. . . . On the return trip Stoddard and Burchard took passage on a Great Lakes steamer and saw the wonders of Niagara before boarding a New York Central train back to Glens Falls.

During the course of the journey the photographer made about a thousand exposures. His greatest disappointment came when he discovered — too late to be able to do anything about it — that his "elephant" camera was a total failure. This huge piece of equipment had been built under his supervision especially for Alaska's scenery and was designed to take a negative measuring 20 x 49½ inches; it was reputed to be the largest

Aged Indian Squaw

Bishop Nicholas of Graeco-Russian Orthodox Church

camera in the world at that time. Run by clockgears the revolving or panoramic lens produced a picture on a curved film that was accurate in perspective and reflective; the result of a quality impossible to obtain in large pictures with a flat plate. Fortunately, the mechanical defects were corrected later on so the innovation was anything but a complete fiasco.

When the mammoth device failed him, Stoddard had to rely on two smaller cameras — a Kodak and another one which took 8 x 10 inch negatives, suitable for lantern slides.

Although the photographer had his pictures, Burchard did not go home empty-handed either. From the mate of the "Quinta," a small coastal steamer, he bought a jet black, four-month-old bear cub named Ned. While he weighed only thirty-five pounds at that time, the small bruin grew fast and put on poundage. He was a very playful pet even though somewhat destructive. Burchard took him to his home in New York City, where he became the subject of a biography written by his master and illustrated by Stoddard, which appeared in a magazine for juveniles.

The Alaska program proved to be one of Stoddard's finest entertainments. Using 150 carefully-tinted slides the opening lecture drew an audience of more than 1,000 people to the Glens Falls Opera House. Since very few Americans had the leisure and the money to travel great distances for pleasure in those days, the slides were fascinating to them. The prairie scenes, the Canadian Mounted Police, the Indians, the Rockies, the Pacific coast towns, the shipboard scenes, the salmon canneries, the gold fields, the glaciers — all these sights were theirs for the evening and held them entranced.

So impressive was the program that the following day a resolution was adopted by the Executive Committee of the Glens Falls Lyceum which sponsored the lecture:

"Resolved, that the stereopticon program given last evening by S. R. Stoddard was so unusually meritorious that we deem it our duty to recommend to the lecturer his entrance upon a wider and more public lecture field.

"The fact that over a thousand people crowded the Opera House while many more were unable to find even standing room, testifies to the high appreciation of the lecturer by his fellow citizens. The close attention of the vast audience was held for nearly three hours under the charm of a natural and conversational delivery, emphasized at times by vivid and eloquent descriptions while the eyes were continually fascinated by choice and artistic views, true to nature as well in color as in outline.

"The whole entertainment was replete with valuable information attractively arranged and delightfully presented."
A. B. Abbott, President
D. C. Farr (Principal, Glens Falls Academy) Secretary
Sherman Williams (Superintendent, Public Schools) Treasurer

126

George B. Gow (Pastor, First Baptist Church) Chairman, Executive Committee

Fenwick M. Cookson, (Rector, Church of the Messiah)

T. A. Sweeney

Charles E. Bullard

Wherever this exciting lecture was given during the years that followed, it proved to be very popular. Apparently this and "The Adirondacks" were two of Stoddard's best programs.

Chapter 11

The Sunny South

It comes as somewhat of a surprise to discover that beating loudly on the publicity drum is not as recent an advertising innovation as one might think. As far back as 70 years a news service in St. Augustine, Florida, was touting that state's appreciable tourist attractions and evinced wideawake awareness of an opportunity when it presented itself. On February 25, 1894 an enterprising word merchant toiling for *The News*, a weekly publication devoted to furthering the interests of Southern resorts, made his appeal in the following logical, sweet-talking fashion:

"*The News* is pleased to announce that the well-known photographer, lecturer and publisher, Mr. S. R. Stoddard of Glens Falls, N. Y., is to make a tour of Florida for the purpose of gathering material for a lecture on 'The Land of Flowers.'

"What is of more immediate interest to the readers of *The News* is the fact that Mr. Stoddard will contribute a series of articles to this journal; bits of Florida travel and virgin impressions which, it is unnecessary to say, will be entertaining features of the issues in which they shall appear.

"Mr. Stoddard's lectures are illustrated by means of a large stereopticon, the pictures for which he makes himself, being a practicing photographer of more than thirty years' experience. Of these pictures Mr. J. B. Pond, under whose management the lectures are given, says," 'Mr. Stoddard's pictures are the most beautiful ever shown before an American audience, and I do not believe that they are equaled in any part of the world!'

"Mr. Stoddard will leave for the South within a few days, reaching Jacksonville by one of the ships of the Clyde Line. He will, as a matter of course, spend some time in St. Augustine, where, it is hoped, our good friends will see that he departs not only with a favorable opinion of this place, but with the most pleasant memories of its hospitality.

"*The News* believes that it will be to the best interest of all those who are interested in Florida to see that Mr. Stoddard is given a cordial welcome and that every means for the collection of material for his proposed lecture be accorded him.

"An illustrated lecture on Florida, given throughout the North next summer and autumn, would be one of the best advertisements Florida could have. But of course it is superfluous to mention this even by way of parenthesis to the hotel and transportation interests of the State.

"For one, *The News* bids Mr. Stoddard welcome and sincerely hopes that his Florida experience may prove to be a Florida Enchantment!"

On this trip, as on all the other longer journeys, Stoddard showed his ingenuity and business acumen. Prior to his departure from Glens Falls, he had already made a deal whereby he got his passage expenses paid for in return for a Clyde Steamship Co., advertisement in his guidebooks. Similar arrangements with the Baltimore & Ohio, the D. & H., the Boston and Maine, the Central Vermont, the Michigan Central, the Chicago and Great Northern, the Canadian National and several other railroad systems minimized his travel costs considerably.

On his trip to Alaska and his three European junkets — to the Mediterranean countries, Egypt and the Near East in 1895; England, Scotland, the North Atlantic islands, Scandinavia and Russia in 1897, and to the Paris Exposition, France and Germany in 1900 — he demonstrated even greater financial skill. In the first two instances he photographed crew and passengers and took orders — and cash pre-payments — for profusely illustrated folio volumes covering the voyages. Priced at $7.00 for the regular edition and $10.00 for the deluxe leather-bound version, these handsome souvenirs not only sold well but also providently furnished all the illustrations needed for numerous lecture programs in later years.

Although the photographer customarily kept clippings and other printed mementos of his travels, for some reason there were fewer of those on Florida than usual. Whereas there are generally at least ten to fifteen press reports relating to each of the other long travels, there are only five that recount his first trip to the Southland. It is known that he left New York in late February and spent the rest of that month and most of March "where summer spends the winter."

As was typical of him he took many pictures of frigid Northern scenes in order to establish the desired contrasts. Among these were those which showed winter along the Hudson and in the great city at its mouth. Charleston and Fort Sumter were next put on film, along with the first few in a long series of photos of the Southern Negroes. Then came Jacksonville, the St. John's River and more pictures of colored people. These were followed by a sequence taken in the vicinity of St. Augustine, where people put out the welcome mat in grand style. Among the subjects were those of Ponce de Leon, ancient and modern; Magnolia Springs Hotel, Spanish moss and Southern roads, Southern forests and their inhabitants and then still more featuring the various types of Florida darkeys.

The steamboat trip up the Oclawaha River to the headwaters of one of its tributaries at Silver Springs was probably one of the scenic highlights of his stay in Florida. The Oclawaha is a sizeable river but the tributary, which meanders for over a hundred miles through an otherwise impenetrable swamp, is so narrow that the excursion boat often brushed against the overhanging trees in passing. Huge alligators were often seen lolling lazily in the brackish water or sunning themselves on logs. Cottonmouths or water moccasins, those deadly, repulsive denizens of the swamplands, were frequently seen hanging from the low trees or slithering through the dark water.

Up this river from Palatka the steamboats ran regularly. Starting early in the afternoon they arrived at Silver Springs the middle of the next morning, picking their way at night by the light of pitch-pine torches, burning in iron jacks on the top of the pilot house. Under the weird light thus provided the colored deckhands sang their immemorial, full-voiced songs.

The Springs themselves must have been even more impressive than now because they had not yet become so commercialized. Instead of a bevy of Bikinied dolls Stoddard and his traveling companions had the more natural attractions to gaze at. Since there were no glass-bottomed boats at the time, ordinary rowboats still answered the purpose of featuring the submarine wonderland under the almost incredibly clear water. In some places a plumb line had recorded eighty feet yet the huge catfish, long-billed gar (a species of swordfish) and giant turtles swimming slowly about in such depths seemed only a few feet below them. The photographer must have had a field day there and on the return trip.

From Palatka, Stoddard headed back to the East Coast again and there saw Ormond and Coquina Beaches, recently started by Flagler and well on their way to becoming choice shore acreage. Since he was now in the Indian River citrus country, S. R. took full advantage of the photographic opportunity and showed every phase of the growth of the orange from blossom to harvest. Staggered cultivation made this possible. Other fruits — the lemon, sapodilla, pineapple and banana — also had their pictures taken, but not necessarily in that part of Florida since the last two cited grow another hundred miles or more to the south.

All the famed Florida scenery was put on film — savannahs, swamps and sand; mangrove, palmetto, cocoanut and royal palms; deer, alligators, razorback hogs; queen birds and egrets; the living sponge and its skeleton.

Also the scenic spots which have since become so popular and yet so alluring to later generations but which were fascinating oddities to the less-traveled people who patronized Stoddard's lectures. To the relatively homebound, Lake Worth, the Royal Poinciana Hotel, the Gulf of Mexico, Key West, sunset on the Gulf Stream and young Negroes diving for nickels were really something to see and dream about actually seeing in person some day. Moreover, since these pictures became painstakingly brilliant colored slides that, when enlarged by the stereopticon device, were almost as large as the stage curtain (30 feet by 30 feet) — well, it's no wonder that the audience "Ohed and ahed" and the reporters wrote glowingly complimentary reports whenever Stoddard's lectures were shown.

From Key West Stoddard went to Havana, where he photographed everything he considered worth such attention. Morro Castle, the harbor, the place where Columbus landed on San Domingo, where the first Mass was said and where he is buried. The bustling city life was duly noted by the camera — the lumbering oxcarts, teams of half a dozen mules driven tandem, milkmen, mounted poultry dealers, truck vendors, Spanish ladies and women who smoked, lottery ticket sellers, convicts and native soldiers.

Next came Oro, where he saw more of the mantilla-wearing and fan-waving aristocratic wives of the hidalgos as well as a palatial cigar factory and a ruined palace.

It is interesting to note that the man from Glens Falls shrewdly and understandably used these photographs as part of still another program — "Soldiering with the Boys of '98." The following year, when he went to Spain and the other Mediterranean countries aboard the "Friesland," he was able to round out the Columbus story in pictures. He was also well prepared to lecture on the background details concerning the Spanish style of colonialism and its impact on Cuba which later resulted in the Spanish-American War.

Stoddard afterward stated that the set of slides made from this journey to the Sunny South was the finest he had ever prepared for the public. The reason of course is easy to understand. All that practically infinite gamut of colorful and strange flora and fauna, the visual charms of that ever-varying and ever-varied semi-tropical winter paradise — yes, probably even the knowledge that he had cheated the rigorous Northern winter out of eight of its least pleasant weeks undeniably made the sojourn in the Southland that much more delightful.

The reaction of one audience, which packed the Town Hall at Saratoga on January 14, 1895, was undoubtedly duplicated on dozens of other occasions whenever and wherever this entertainment was given. The gist of the reporter's verdict was as follows: "The first of the series of stereopticon lectures by S. R. Stoddard for the benefit of our public schools was given Monday evening before a large and enthusiastic audience. Mr. Stoddard is a pleasing speaker, whose manner and speech are those of a gentleman and student. He is utterly devoid of the charlatanry of the average traveling lecturer. His material was prepared from personal observations and his pictures were what "The Sunny South" is — magnificent!"

This turned out to be the first of many trips south for Stoddard because it is a matter of record that during the seasons of 1900-1903 he was on the staff of the Florida Chautauqua located at De Funiak Springs. The author of the advertising brochure put out by that prestigious organization described S. R. in this manner: "Mr. Stoddard has won wide recognition not only in his own state (New York) as an outstanding illustrated lecturer but also along the Ohio and among the best Chautauquas of our country. No finer pictures have ever been presented on the screen and he will be

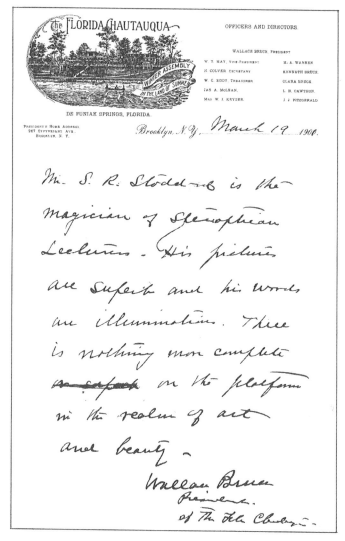

THE FLORIDA CHAUTAUQUA

WINTER ASSEMBLY IN THE LAND OF SUMMER

OFFICERS AND DIRECTORS.

WALLACE BRUCE, PRESIDENT

W. T. MAY, VICE-PRESIDENT   M. A. WARREN

N. COLVER, SECRETARY   KENNETH BRUCE

W. C. EDDY, TREASURER   CLARA BRUCE.

JAS A. McLEAN.   L. R. CAWTHON.

MRS W. J. KRYGER.   J. J. FITZGERALD

DE FUNIAK SPRINGS, FLORIDA.

PRESIDENT'S HOME ADDRESS,
267 STUYVESANT AVE.,
BROOKLYN, N. Y.

Brooklyn, N.Y., March 19, 1900.

Mr. S. R. Stoddard is the magician of Stereoptican Lectures. His pictures are superb and his words are illuminations. There is nothing more complete ~~so perfect~~ on the platform in the realm of art and beauty —

Wallace Bruce
President.
of The Fla Chautauqua —

Wallace Bruce letter

welcomed again with acclamation."

According to the program listing his lectures covered the following subjects: The Pictured Adirondacks; America's Wonderland (Yellowstone, Grand Canyon of the Colorado, the Yosemite); Alaska, The Land of Ice; Across the Continent; The Sunny South; Cuba Liber; Egypt and the Nile; The Land of Christ; Europe's Odd Corners and The Midnight Sun.

A reporter for *The Daily Breeze*, the De Funiak Springs local paper, had this reaction to Stoddard's "Wonderland" program: "Nothing better could be said of Mr. Stoddard's third lecture than to say that it was as good as the first two. Indeed nothing better could be said of any illustrated lecture than to say it was as good as Stoddard's."

Hon. Wallace Bruce, president of the Florida Chautauqua, evaluated Stoddard's series in this statement: "S. R. Stoddard is a wide traveler, a rich humorist and an unrivaled artist. His pictures are superb and his words are illuminations. There is nothing more complete on the lecture platform in the realm of art and beauty."

Fred Emerson Brooks, the jovial poet of the Golden State, who saw one of Stoddard's lectures on California described his slides as "the most beautiful pictures I have ever seen. The coloring is exquisite. I have seen the pictures and the pictured so I know."

Stoddard's southern engagements as well as those given elsewhere were under the management of the Star Lyceum Bureau and Maj. J. B. Pond, both of New York City. A sound idea of his status as a speaker can be drawn from glancing at the list of Pond's other clients, among whom were such notables as Dr. Lyman Abbott, Dr. Felix Adler, Poultney Bigelow, George W. Cable, Dr. William Drummond, John Fox, Jr., Julia Ward Howe, Elbert Hubbard, Hamilton Wright Mabie, Ernest Seton-Thompson, Dr. Henry van Dyke and Woodrow Wilson.

Fairly convincing evidence that the man from Glens Falls must have had quite an array of arrows in his quiver, and that his skill as a speaker was obviously not his least effective talent.

Chapter 12

Across The Continent

On September 21, 1894, Stoddard left Glens Falls on a transcontinental trip which took him on an S-shaped tour that covered in all nearly 10,000 miles (450 of it by stage) before his return to his starting point 47 days later. The Yellowstone Park formed the head of the letter S; Butte, Montana, the turn to the south; Salt Lake, the bend eastward; the Garden of the Gods, the downward turn; thence westward to the Grand Canyon of the Colorado and the Pacific coast.

The first stop on his itinerary was at Niagara Falls, where he spent a day at the American and Canadian reservations, Whirlpool Rapids, on the 'Maid of the Mist' and in the 'Cave of the Winds.' All of these attractions were put on film.

From Niagara Falls he continued his trip on the Michigan Central, the only railroad which passed close to the cataract and which made it a point to stop so that its passengers could get a good view. The same place, according to Stoddard, that Frederick Church used as the vantage point for his masterpiece now in the Corcoran Art Gallery in Washington, D. C.

In the Windy City, he boarded the Chicago, Milwaukee and St. Paul line with a stopover at the Wisconsin Dells to photograph that scenic spot before resuming the journey along picturesque Lake Pepin to St. Paul. From there, via the Northern Pacific Railroad, he went through Minnesota and the Bad Lands of the Dakotas to Livingston, Montana. At this town he left the main line for a week's visit to the Yellowstone National Park.

Gardiner City, on the edge of this great Park, was noteworthy for two reasons — its saloons and its cemetery. The latter had seven occupants at the time, five of whom were "gentlemen who happened to be a little slow with their guns. The other two corpses had formerly been absent-minded individuals who had made the mistake of spot-requisitioning horses which had not belonged to them — and had been subsequently "interviewed" by the citizens.

The Yellowstone wonderland seemed to him to be a region of contradictions: "Strata of rock formed under water and glacial drift are mixed as if the conditions which produced them existed at the same time. You went in with a theory to account for everything and came out with all your theories shattered." The Mammoth Hot Springs Hotel and a number of buildings occupied by government soldiers stationed there to guard the preserve were situated on a plateau built up by extinct hot springs. Active springs built terraces at the rate of half an inch a month. The red, orange, white and blue which he saw in the steaming springs were noted and later were matched on the tinted slides.

Stages required five days to make the circuit of the Park's attractions, among them a newly-made beaver dam, a mountain of volcanic glass — and Larry, the man of gall who welcomed the travelers and overcharged them for the cold comforts of his lunch tent at Norris Basin.

The numerous geysers of course absorbed his interest. The Grotto, the Fan, the Castle, the Monarch — and Old Faithful's clock-like performance — all these natural wonders, the brilliantly-colored rock formations and Yellowstone Falls, 360 feet high, delighted this artist and provided provender for many exceptional photographs. . .

A short stay in the silver and copper mining city of Butte, then on to Salt Lake City, whose wide streets, electric street cars and considerate conductors impressed S. R. favorably. He visited the Tabernacle, capacity 9,000, while a conference was in session and gazed on several hundred real live Mormons. He saw where Brigham Young began his housekeeping, then crossed the river Jordan and went out to Great Salt Lake, one of the resorts where the "Salters" go as New Yorkers did to Coney Island or Long Branch. The buoyant effect of the salt water and the salt heaps awaiting shoveling up for marketing aroused his curiosity and attention.

From Salt Lake his journey was eastward on the Rio Grande R. R. to Grand Junction, Colorado. The railroad wound through some fearfully wild mountain gorges, then over the Continental Divide at 11,000 feet and down to Leadville, which had seen some of the craziest crazes ever experienced in gold mining. This mountain metropolis was to him an odd mixture of modern buildings and miners' shacks which people had to bend over nearly double to enter. Log-sided and round-roofed, they seemed more like dog kennels than human habitations. All the surrounding hills and valleys were pierced with tunnels and showed piles of dirt around their entrances like sand around ant hills.

Crossing Hagerman Pass, west of Leadville, the Sante Fe railroad took the photographer through some of the country's most spectacular scenery to Colorado Springs, a slight disappointment because it was on the plains. The side streets, the imposing houses set in ample yards made a very favorable impression on Stoddard which somewhat offset his unfavorable reaction to Manitou Springs and the Garden of the Gods. The unheated cars on the cog railroad to Pike's Peak and the plethora of saloons did not appeal to him. He considered the Garden to be anything but that and its 240 acres of strange, blood-red limestone shapes, although impressive and

Characteristic Pueblo Houses

Indian Peddlers and Their Customers

worth seeing, suggestive of a crude joke. A sign announcing lots for sale compounded the crudity.

The next place of interest on his itinerary was Laguna, the home of the Pueblo Indians and also the mesa-topped villages and cliff dwellings of their ancestors. There were about 300 Indians in Laguna at the time, occasionally served by a priest from the Catholic church built by Spaniards over 200 years previously, but for the most part observing the ceremonies of their own ancient religion with its special gods for nearly every time and condition.

A school teacher provided by the Government had been unable to accomplish much toward educating the children. Although she had already been there for nearly four years, the elders of the tribe did not see the necessity for the white man's system of education and therefore did not force their children to attend. The latter of course found it far more congenial to wallow in the dirt.

The Pueblos were, however, a colorful people. The broad-brimmed white hats, the gaily-colored shirts and beaded moccasins of the men and the bright-colored shawls and blankets and numerous silver ornaments of the women later on were duplicated on slides.

Moreover, he was further impressed by their industry: the men as farmers and herdsmen; the women as weavers, water carriers and pottery makers.

From Laguna, Stoddard went on to Flagstaff, Arizona, already an important cattle town, railroad station and wide-open frontier mecca for cowboys and gamblers. It was also the point of departure for the seventy-three mile stagecoach ride to the Grand Canyon of the Colorado. The bone-bruising trip, with the Easterner as the only passenger, lasted for twelve long hours. It started out with a spirited team of mules doing the hauling. These were later replaced at intervals by three relays of horses.

To him Arizona was a country in the sky; the level was higher than the highest Adirondack peaks. A great, high, arid plain with no living streams and little rain, a land of terrific thunder and lightning storms and very few precious springs, it acted as a fitting preliminary for the Canyon itself.

He spent two days there — one in tramping a distance of ten miles along the rim and another in the descent to the river. With a guide accompanying him they rode on mules two-thirds of the way and then walked the rest over the trail originally built to reach a copper mine about halfway down. The guide did not seem overjoyed but Stoddard felt that it would be humiliating to have come so far (nearly 3,000 miles) and then stop two or three miles short of the goal — so the guide went on. On the return trip the guide told him that he was the first tourist ever to go all the way down to the river. It was a strenuous day's work, and one that left him almost a wreck, as he put it. But when they finally returned to the upper world, he called it the experience of a lifetime.

138

Probably Stoddard in Canyon

The huge gorge, more than thirteen miles from rim to rim, filled with red and yellow mountains and nearly a mile and a half deep, cut into long lateral canyons, domes, spires and minarets — all these stupendous phenomena left Stoddard speechless while he let his camera record the wonders for future audiences to marvel at. The sunset scenes, the moonlight on the cliffs and the firelight streaming from the cabin windows of the lodge made memorable photographs which fascinated all who saw them.

A day later found him on his way to something green and watery — southern California and Old Mexico, then Los Angeles; then San Diego and later still the Yosemite. Its gigantic trees, mighty cliffs and hanging waterfalls were to him beautiful beyond description. He passed an eventful week there and among the Mariposa big trees and the old Spanish missions. He wondered at the control of the old padres over the natives to get them to do labor which had no parallel perhaps since the children of Israel labored under their Egyptian taskmasters.

In San Francisco he took sunset views of the Golden Gate, moonlight views of the Pacific out over Seal Rocks and several of Chinatown, whose inhabitants he considered cowardly and spiritless but indispensable as workers and house servants. Generally inoffensive he considered them

139

and based this opinion on observations through open doors which showed the most depraved tastes possible. These pagans seemed to Stoddard to be satisfied with wrecking themselves body and soul.

From San Francisco he traveled northward through California, Oregon and Washington to Tacoma, where he headed east again over the Northern Pacific Railroad and back to Glens Falls.

He had taken over 700 negatives of the trip as well as color notes and studies of the more important subjects. Just the tinting of the 150 selected slides required weeks of concentrated effort before Stoddard felt that that phase of the projected lecture was ready. The accompanying descriptive commentary also required painstaking preparation.

Since he had not yet completed work on the "Sunny South" material compiled the preceding Spring, that program was given priority attention. Therefore it was not until March 25th the next year that "America's Wonderland" was first given as an illustrated lecture and still later, as "Across the Continent," appeared in manuscript form although it was never published.

For that Glens Falls audience the pictures were a revelation, "They were," according to a report for the Glens Falls *Morning Star,* "as of an unknown country with peculiarities of form and color strange to Eastern eyes and almost challenging belief. . . . The grouping of the series of widely-differing views in one evening's entertainment gives a clear idea of their relative claims and it is found that each is essentially different from the other. Each is complete in itself. The Yellowstone represents mystery, a world in the process of creation. The Grand Canyon, unearthly grandeur. The Yosemite, beauty beyond compare. Truly, "America's Wonderland" is the wonderland of the world. The views embodied splendid coloring and the narrator exhibited remarkable descriptive ability. A wonderful evening for all fortunate enough to be in attendance."

On March 15, 1901, when the same program was given in De Funiak Springs, Florida, a reporter described the entertainment as follows: " 'Wonderland' is a fitting title for Mr. Stoddard's lecture on the gorgeous scenery of Yellowstone Park, the Grand Canyon and the Yosemite. The slides are works of art worthy of some of our greatest modern painters. In his verbal descriptions Mr. Stoddard is never monotonous nor tautological. He is a thorough and enthusiastic lecturer and artist — a rare combination in this age of hurry and superficial display."

Chapter 13

Stoddard's Northern Monthly

Nearly all the leading magazines of the past century have carried occasional articles on the Adirondacks, but only three periodicals were
nominally devoted to advancing its interests. First in the field was *Woods
and Waters,* started in 1898 by the supercharged, eighteen-year-old Harry
V. Radford of New York City. Successful from its very start the modest
four-page brochure burgeoned into a thirty-page quarterly within two
years and soon boasted a circulation of 20,000.

Much of this was directly traceable to the persuasiveness, aggressive-
ness and energy of its founder, whose personal popularity attracted profitable advertising and well-known contributors of content material. Moreover, he also had the enthusiastic support of the Adirondack hotelmen and
guides, a potent asset in itself.

Although the direct and indirect advertising usually shared more than
equal space with the articles, a sign of solvency in publishing, the color
illustrations, usually by Kemp, were excellent. The photographs, however,
were seldom as professional as those which enhanced Stoddard's magazine. Regrettably too, far too many of the articles were set in areas other
than the Adirondacks.

Radford's editorial energies were focused mainly on the introduction
of animals once native to the Adirondacks, but which had since been ex-
terminated. His successive crusades restored the beaver permanently and
the moose and elk temporarily. He also was the principal proponent and
persistent lobbying force behind the passage of legislation creating a
closed season on the black bear.

In 1905, after the death of his mother, Radford suddenly decided to
stop publication and concentrate on his long-deferred desire to hunt and
explore to his heart's content. This he did until, in 1912, his life and
that of Thomas G. Street, his like-minded companion, were terminated by
Eskimo spears following a tragic misunderstanding with their guides on
the lonely shores of the Canadian Arctic.

Forest Leaves, the second Adirondack-oriented magazine, made its
appearance in 1903. Also a quarterly this little periodical was superior in

every respect and richly deserved its widespread popularity. Founded by Sister Mary Kieran of the Sanitarium Gabriels, it was "written by friends of the Adirondacks to be read by friends of the Adirondacks" and it added much to the literary lore of the region.

The first five years of its existence were its best years as far as the quality of the articles was concerned. Radford, Murray, Stoddard, Stevenson and Stewart E. White and other writers were among the contributors during the period.

From 1907 until the cessation of publication in 1934, *Forest Leaves* had a considerable circulation.

The *Northern Monthly,* Stoddard's publication, got off to an auspicious start in May, 1906. Designed to fill the gap left by Radford's decision to leave the field, it was a very impressive, full-fledged issue containing many articles and eye-pleasing illustrations, including a three-tone picture of Marcy, all taken by the noted photographer.

In the foreword S. R. Stoddard stated his editorial philosophy as follows: "The fundamental policy of the *Northern Monthly* will be the gathering and preservation of unrecorded stories and traditions of the Great North Woods; to picture with pen and camera the glories of its mountains and valleys; to present their worthy features, and in all legitimate ways to advance the interests of Northern New York. Illustrations will be given lavishly, for pictures talk, and the camera cannot tell a lie.

"The effort will be made to get at the truth concerning unsettled questions affecting the welfare of place and people and present it for consideration.

"The public domain is being despoiled and the rights of coming generations jeopardized for private gain. Do the people realize this?

"The little thieves are being punished and the big ones presented with bouquets. Why?

"If you have a word to say for the public good, a good story of hunting or fishing, or a tradition that is worth preserving, send it in. The invitation is for all who mean well."

The first issue led off with a Stoddard article and photos of Marcy and environs. Succeeding copies also contained many items pertaining to the Adirondacks, but Donaldson was right when he commented that there was much extraneous matter — foreign travel, fiction and poetry. Apparently, in addition to its avowed purpose of furthering the cause of the Great North Woods, this magazine was also directed toward other and broader reader interests.

Obviously, even for a man younger than 63, it would have been a formidable task to find enough exclusively northern New York items to fill the space requirements. At that time — and even now — there just wasn't enough worthwhile material available for a periodical to concentrate solely on Adirondackana.

Therefore, it is easy to understand why the aging editor, who had a *monthly not a quarterly* deadline to meet, felt it both urgent and advisable to use his Far Western and European travel experiences to full advantage. Moreover and probably for the same reason, he gladly accepted the earlier work of emerging authors and added drama, fashion and current architecture departments. The writers got the recognition and he got the needed material, a mutually satisfactory arrangement.

The June, 1906 copy certainly more than made up for the first issue's deficiency in upstate lore, because it contained many literary and pictorial delights. Following a tinted photo depicting a passing storm over Lower Ausable Lake, there came an excellent description of Keene Valley by S. R. S.; a short history of the Ausable Club (St. Hubert's) by Edwin Howell, one of its officers; an interesting account of the Glenmore Summer School by Stephen Weston, Dean of Antioch College. Next came Harry Radford's "Elk in the Adirondacks;" H. D. Kellogg's "Mitchell Sabattis" and Henry van Hoevenbergh's "Forsaken Village." Interspersed were five Stoddard photos of Keene Valley and the Ausable Lakes.

July, 1906 must have been a visual treat for the many lovers of Lake George and Lake Champlain, for its frontispiece photo of Dome Island with its picturesque backdrop of clouds and mountains was followed by historical accounts of each lake and enhanced by nineteen illustrations, including a map. An added attraction was H. V. Radford's "Return of the Beaver."

August, 1906 had a colored Indian Pass picture for a frontispiece. Included in the contents were van Hoevenbergh's poetic phantasy, "The Legend of the Indian Pass;" John Carlstrom's "The Hermit's Secret" (Elizabethtown setting), Stoddard's article on the Adirondacks, a map showing railroad and stage routes to the mountains, photos of Marcy and Lake Tear of the Clouds, Bartlett's, W. W. Durant's Camp Pine Knot and an Upper Ausable Lake open camp or lean-to.

September, 1906 opened with an eye-arresting picture of Avalanche Lake; this was followed by photos of lumberjacks at work, the Boreas region, a winter scene in the Adirondacks, Lake Tear of the Clouds from the south and two maps. The first of these showed the St. Lawrence and Hudson River drainage systems; the second chart showed the northern counties with the State Park area also indicated. "Champlain's Battle with the Iroquois," by S.R.S.; "A Simple Adirondack Tale" by A. A. Young and "The North Country," a poem by Cornelia Brown, accounted for the rest of that issue's Adirondack items.

October, 1906 led off with "The Pottersville Fair," a clever satirical piece by Stoddard. The first installment of a series called "Old Times in the Adirondacks," also appeared that month. Written by the author for use in his guidebooks, the thirteen episodes form a narrative of his trip to the wilderness in 1873. His amusing handling of some somewhat exasperating people and situations earned for Stoddard an enviable place among American humorists of that era.

The November, 1906 issue had a very effective frontispiece — Drowned Lands of the Raquette, depicting the desolation caused by the periodic opening and closing of the lumbermen's storage dams. The only other Adirondack pieces were the second part of "Old Times in the Adirondacks" and "In the Starlight," a poem by van Hoevenbergh.

The December, 1906 issue of course concentrated on the Christmas theme and featured religious articles and numerous photographs taken by Stoddard in the Holy Land ten years previously. Two of the three articles — "Il Santissimo Bambino" and "The First Christmas" — were written by Stoddard and show profound spiritual insight. The third and equally moving narrative, called "In His Footsteps," was by Samuel Jacob. Part 3 of "Old Times in the Adirondacks" also was included.

The reason for analyzing the contents of the first eight issues of the *Northern Monthly* is to show that its readers were not exactly short-changed. Besides the articles cited there were of course many other stories to round out the usual 85-100 pages.

A potent factor in the success of the first year of publication was the hard-hitting nature of the editorials. Stoddard expressed his satisfaction with his efforts in these words: "With this issue the *Northern Monthly* completes its first volume. Its excuse for coming was the call of stripped mountains and complaining forests, voiceless, yet speaking mightily to the eye in shrinking streams and sudden floods.

"The public domain was being despoiled for private gain. The little thieves were punished, the big ones given seats of honor. There was a well-organized attempt to disrupt the Forest Preserve by greedy lumber, pulp and power interests thinly veiled under a plea of philanthropy and for the public good. As a means to this end the country was being flooded with articles sent out as "News from Albany," advocating the adoption of the Malby-Merritt amendment as a necessity in water storage for the suppression of floods and for the industrial advancement of the river towns. It came within the province of the *Northern Monthly* to expose the unfair character of these half-truths. . . .In the controversy truths have been spoken when friends advised diplomacy, facts given when policy suggested silence, and things called by their proper names until the anonymous authors of the misleading articles uncovered in their own defense and stood revealed as the brazen agents of the lumber, pulp and power interests conniving to get something for nothing regardless of the people's vested rights.

"It is believed that the *Northern Monthly* has come to stay. A steadily expanding subscription list with an increasing demand for sale indicate growing approval.

"The policy is unchanged: there will be outspoken criticism of everything threatening the integrity of the Adirondacks, the same general course in the gathering and publication of unpublished stories and traditions of the Great North Woods, and the picturing of mountains and valleys as in the past. . ."

During the second year Stoddard, in order to meet increased expenses, published his magazine in a pocket-size edition. He also spelled out what he personally advocated as being "for the good of the Adirondacks." This creed consisted of the following five tenets:

1) "I am thoroughly in favor of storage reservoirs for regulating the flow of the Hudson, but they should be outside the State Park and no opportunity given for the destruction of the forests in the construction of dams therefor."

2) "I would have a law to prohibit the cutting of trees on land drained by the Hudson River one thousand feet above tide, regardless of ownership. If any man were injured thereby, the State could well afford to pay the value of the trees left standing.

3) "I would have the State control absolutely to the rim the Hudson River watershed in the interests of the people of the cities along its course who must soon look to the mountains for water to drink. It is immaterial who owns the land so long as the woods and waters are preserved under inviolable laws.

4) "I would have the State control all the undeveloped water power along the Hudson's tributaries in the interests of equity and charge consumers a fair price based on the cost of construction and maintenance. It should not come into competition with private interests except to the extent of preventing a monopoly which might withhold from small consumers the opportunity to obtain power at a fair price. It should not deprive established interests of acquired rights on land or in the ordinary flow of the river, but could justly make consumers with water power of their own pay a fair portion for water furnished in excess of the ordinary flow in times of scarcity.

5) "Preservation of the forests as a matter of sentiment recognizes no boundaries, but from a utilitarian point of view the territory drained by the Hudson River is of infinitely greater value to the State and to the world at large than all other Adirondack territory whose waters run in other directions."

These enlightened, forthright policy guideposts won for the author strong support as well as bitter opposition. Probably his staunchest assistance came from Clarence L. Parker, of Norwich, N. Y., who contributed three powerful articles to the cause. The first, in the April, 1907 issue, called "Adirondack Forest Lands," was a potent piece of straight thinking and writing based on Charles A. Lincoln's *Constitutional History of New York.* He followed this up with "Who's Who in the Water Storage Deal?" in the June, 1907 issue. This time he identified the legislators and lobbyists with the interests they really represented. The third attack, which appeared in August, 1907, was entitled "The Water Question — Present

Condition." This reviewed progress in the critical arena of antagonistic interests and closed with this irrefutable statement: "These results have been accomplished by honest influence, an honest Governor (Hughes) and work done by the Board of Trade of New York City, the Association for the Protection of the Adirondacks and individual workers for the good of the Adirondacks. . . .The average man is an honest man. He wants to be honest with you and me, he wants us to be honest with each other and he wants all men to be honest with the State. Show him the honest side of any question and he is glad to go with it."

It is interesting to note that both the powerful organizations mentioned in the Parker piece sent letters to Stoddard which gave him a share of the credit for the legislative victories.

The summer issues of 1907 contained generously-illustrated articles on Lake Champlain, Saratoga and Ausable Chasm, besides continuing the series called *Old Times in the Adirondacks.*

The September, 1907 number was outstanding because of his Adirondack Murray tribute, Murray's letter to C. H. Bennett of the Antlers, Raquette Lake; and Adirondack Harry Radford's letter to Stoddard praising the *Northern Monthly.*

Stoddard's eulogy of Murray, who had died on March 4, 1904, is brief but eloquent: "To Adirondack Murray the mountains owe much. His *Adventures in the Wilderness* created an enthusiasm in thousands that led them into the wilds. It wrought a splendid record in those who followed with understanding, and sad havoc to the callow, misled by the magic of his fertile pen. The things of which he wrote were far from spiritual, and not for weaklings, but so attractive that weaklings followed and fell. He was an ardent fisherman for both fish and men and most attractive his lures, but no manly man ever laid the blame for discomforts into which he was led on the sturdy idealist who carried the vital energy of splendid youth under the misleading shadow of his snowy head. His teachings were of sport, but his nature was of good will and sympathy and wholesome helpfulness, of love of his fellow man and of Nature's ways."

A few years before his death, at a time when most of his former confidence had waned, Murray wrote these moving words to a friend: "How hateful it is to age into weakness and loss of power! To say of each flower, 'It is the last time I shall see it bloom,' and to each star that shines 'Soon I shall see it no more.' Get Mamelons and read Atlas' testimony at the funeral of the chief: 'Oh Death, how I hate thee!' Do you know that she stands to me as the type of us all? I do not ever expect to find a world so beautiful as this, or men so gentle and generous or women so sweet and good. I have always been so human and I thank God for it!"

The following eloquently revealing letter from Murray to Charles Bennett, hotelman of Raquette Lake, was also printed in the same issue (September 1907) of the *Northern Monthly:*

"My dear Mr. Bennett:

I am very sorry that we did not meet again before I left town — as we expected — for in a few moments certain important details might have been arranged and a mutual understanding regarding them arrived at. One or two points I will suggest:

In the case of the Adirondacks certain peculiarities stand out. In most cases the railroads and hotels are first built and then they join hands in "booming" the region to which they wish to attract attention and travel. Vast sums of money are spent year after year to draw the people there. Sometimes they succeed — sometimes they do not.

But in the case of the Adirondacks — the most popular summer resort in the country and the one best known throughout the world — it was not advertised or made popular in that way. It is not immodest for me to state the fact, and the fact is that one volume — purely literary, published by the most select publication house in the country at that time, and a lecture by the author of the book, made the wilderness famous and sent thousands into it.

The lecture has not received the credit, as a promoting force, that it deserves, for it was delivered over 500 times during the three years subsequent to the publication of the book, and nearly if not quite half a million of the educated and wealthy people of New England and New York state listened to it and were influenced by it.[1] The result was that long before railroad facilities were provided to transport the people to the woods swiftly and in comfort, or hotels were built and furnished to accommodate them, a vast and profitable patronage was provided them. For years the demand for accommodations far exceeded the supply.

And all this was accomplished by two purely literary efforts — one in the form of a book, the other a literary lecture which reached the people from the Lyceum platform — without the cost of a cent to the lines of transportation or to the parties who built the hotels and cottages.

In the light of these facts it seems to me evident that the forces that were adequate thirty years ago are adequate still. If I undertake to add to what I have done, I shall follow, in producing what I may produce, the same line of influence on the public mind that was proven so effective then.

It has been in my mind for some years to revisit the woods, to produce another volume and prepare another address on the Adirondacks of today in the same popular vein as the old one. But I do not ask or wish any financial assistance or consideration for doing this from any party or parties. I wish to and do here acknowledge the friendly appreciation and hospitable spirit shown me at our conference in New York recently, but I do not feel that it would be becoming for me to accept any help even from you and Mr. (Paul) Smith — whom

I most highly esteem — save such incidental courtesies as men in friendly relationships may properly and are accustomed to extend to each other.

But touching the circulation of my published works, to which you both allude, I welcome any assistance you can without inconvenience give me. It seems to me entirely proper that the hotels of the Adirondacks should have these volumes in their libraries and free for their guests to read, for they are of a nature to entertain those who love outdoor life and frequent the woods where the scenes of many of the stories were laid and of which, as the years go on, they will be more and more influential advertisement.

At least that is my expectation as it is my hope. For when all my doing is done and my life's work ended, it is probable that my best and most lasting influence for good among men will be found in my efforts to make men and women love and appreciate outdoor life and admire the simplicity and nobleness of those whose characters were most influenced by it.

Writing in the spirit of frankness to Mr. Smith and yourself, I would say that I should be pleased if my works were in every hotel in the woods. But I do not see any way in which I myself can move directly in the matter, so I must leave the initiative wholly to your good offices.

Truly yours,
W. H. H. Murray

Murray Homestead, Guilford, Conn.
April 4, 1901.

P.S. This communication in substance has been forwarded by this same mail to Mr. Smith, with whom you may consult.

M."

Supplemental to Murray's letter was the following to Stoddard by Harry V. Radford, Murray's enthusiastic biographer and chief promoter of the Adirondack Murray Memorial Association. Wrote Radford:

"It may interest you to know that the tour of the Adirondacks Mr. Murray was then planning was to be taken in company with myself. We were to travel through the Adirondacks together and then go on a speaking tour of the State — a campaign for the Adirondack Park and forest preservation. I was to accompany him everywhere, introduce him on the platform and, as he termed it, act as his understudy. I had no doubt that I could learn something of the art of delivery by such close contact with this master of oratory and persuasion.

---

1. In Radford's brief *Adirondack Murray*, (p. 76) the author states that his mentor-hero received from $100 to $500 per lecture, thus providing a sound criterion of Murray's fame and speaking skill.

"Unfortunately, soon after Mr. Murray wrote the letter in question, his health failed seriously, and he never afterward became strong enough to undertake either the trip or the speaking campaign. Had he been able to carry out the plans, I have no doubt that ere this the Adirondack Park would have been realized, for we planned to carry the campaign everywhere — the floors of the Legislature included — and Mr. Murray's ringing appeals would have carried everything before him.

"Another plan, which also had to fail because of Mr. Murray's poor health, was the establishment of a literary Adirondack Magazine (not unlike your *Northern Monthly* in scope) devoted to the preservation of the Adirondacks, of which he was to be the editor and I assistant editor. Your magazine, however, has since filled the field most creditably.

"It will surely please you to know that there is a distinct Adirondack Murray revival setting in. Unusual interest in his books is being manifested on all sides, and they are selling better than for several years. It is remarkable how his first book, *Adventures in the Wilderness,* keeps its hold upon the public. After nearly forty years of steady sale it is still being printed at regular intervals by its publisher (De Wolfe & Fiske Co. of Boston). All of his other books sell well too. His widow sells a good many every year. She has an edition of her own — independent from the De Wolf edition.

Yours truly,
Radford"

North Creek, N. Y. Aug. 24, 1907

Probably the most controversial subject which occupied Stoddard's editorial attention was concerned with deer hunting and its annual grim toll of human life. Hoping to eliminate such senseless seasonal slaughter he staunchly advocated the return of legal hounding of the deer, a method he deplored which had been outlawed in 1902 after a seven-year trial period.

As a boy he had fully shared in that very natural delight in killing which riots in the breast of nearly every male. Then, one day in the woods he suddenly came practically face to face with a big doe running before the dogs. He shot, the deer went down, but her big eyes which looked into his haunted him for many a day and night thereafter. That was his first and last deer and understandably he agreed with those who came to think that pursuit with dogs was cruel and unworthy of a true sportsman. He continued to believe so and was very willing that the law which grew out of a sentiment of pity for the deer should be retained in its interests and as a means of keeping the inexperienced hunters out of the woods.

He soon became convinced, however, that the misery caused by still-hunting fatalities should be stopped and his deep conviction became a crusade.

Friends more frank than complimentary warned him that his stand was doing him no good. Since he was no hunter himself, he was butting in where he had no business to do so. According to them sportsmen knew what they wanted and he was only making his magazine extremely unpopular in quarters where he should look for support.

Stoddard refused to yield or to compromise. He insisted that although deforestation has to do with children yet to come, the sins of still-hunting affect the wives and children of today. Was it for the best interests of the Adirondacks that no word should be said against a law that costs the lives of many men to perpetuate a sport?

He declared that in nearly every instance the deaths were caused not by accidents in the handling of guns but by experts who, in the nerve-straining excitement of still-hunting, could not wait to determine for certain that what they fancied must be a deer was not a man. In the days of hounding such mistakes were unknown.

Two other people, among others, shared Stoddard's stand on this matter. One was Justice Henry D. Kellogg of Long Lake, Hamilton County, who wrote:

"I can remember when no such thing was heard of as a man being shot for a deer. . . .As an individual I do not believe in the use of dogs to hunt deer, but it has come to that point where the Legislature should do something to stop the needless sacrifice of human life. In my opinion the only way it can be done is to allow the use of dogs."

Further support came from Fred Smith of Blue Mountain Lake:

"I am with you hand and heart about the game law. It's a bad one as it stands. No life is safe during the hunting season. I know personally that every hunting season is a period of great anxiety to the guides and their families. And how easy it is to kill an enemy during the hunting season!

" 'My God, I've killed a man!' is all there is to it.

"At least the law should be amended so as to imprison for five to ten years anyone who shoots and kills another person. I read what Mr. Church, secretary of the Brown's Tract Guides Association, wrote about inexperienced hunters. But who does the killing, pray? In nearly every case it is the best guides and sportsmen who do it.' "

At a mass meeting called at Blue Mountain Lake on Mar. 21, 1908, ninety-one men, including the writer of the above letter, protested against the continuance of the game laws in their existing form. Representing almost the entire voting population of that mountain community, they adopted a resolution in favor of "Hounding" as a means of protecting human life as against the unguarded dangers of still-hunting. It was an uprising by those most deeply interested against a senseless law, enacted in the name of compassion for the beast and continued in the interest of sportsmen who would hold the royal amusement of deer-killing above the reach of the unskilled regardless of the consequences.

In spite of such ardent efforts the law remained substantially the same and the crusade was unsuccessful.

The valedictory issue of the comparatively short-lived magazine was published in September, 1908. With it Stoddard reluctantly quit the field. "It appeared at a time when such as it aimed to do seemed needed. It worked conscientiously to meet an obvious need with full hope and the belief that support would be given for its necessities. That such recognition did not come from the mass is not said complainingly but only in explanation. Words of commendation from the appreciative few have eased the position and much was done enthusiastically for the love of the cause. But kind words are not accepted as current exchange for paper and printing when payday comes.

"The burden was heavy but it has been cheerfully borne. It is laid down now with infinite regret and only as a matter of necessity after the amount dedicated to the work has been exhausted and physical endurance strained to the limit in an effort to carry this along with other absolutely necessary work, often to the neglect of what some would consider more important duties.

"It is not laid aside carelessly or without effort to have it continued, for there is need and it was believed that arrangements had been made to have the *Monthly* continued by other worthy and more capable hands. But, at the last moment, business sense won out and the almost-persuaded philanthropist decided against it.

"Suggestions as to changes of policy and inducements under other conditions have been offered, but consistency is a jewel. Better honorable failure than a questionable success. The *Adirondack Monthly* goes down with its boots on and its face to the foe."

Such unswerving adherence to principles and high-minded unwillingness to compromise are rarely encountered in any era. Exponents of dedication to such concepts of personal responsibility and duty seldom fail to arouse mixed and critical reactions. Most people would consider Stoddard to have been quixotic, tactless and more than slightly impractical in his brief career as a magazine editor and publisher.

There are, however, probably just as many people whose admiration and appreciation far outweigh their wonder at his seeming lack of business acumen. They wonder how a man who was so successful as a photographer, lecturer, guidebook writer, mapmaker and author should be so relatively unsuccessful as the publisher of a periodical.

Whatever their final opinion may be the fact remains that the *Northern Monthly,* while it was hardly a financial success, was nevertheless eminently successful otherwise. Its wealth of photos, its slashing editorials against timber theft, land grabs, the waste of the State's natural resources, the misuse of public trust and senseless laws, its stories and poems by van Hoevenbergh, W. L. Stone, Stoddard and others and especially noteworthy — the series by Stoddard called "Old Times in the Adirondacks" — all these have and will form — when they are more widely known — a valuable contribution to the literary lore of the Adirondack region.

Chapter 14

The Family Circle

Stoddard family composite

Although his various travels, photographing and lecture tours required his absence at frequent intervals, Stoddard apparently had a reasonably pleasant family life. In 1868, four years after his arrival in Glens Falls, he met, fell in love with and married Helen Augusta Potter. She was a rather

Mrs. Helen Stoddard

Self portrait of Seneca Ray Stoddard (1844-1917)

large woman with a hearty laugh and a pronounced sense of humor. Since Stoddard also was usually inclined to see and appreciate life's lighter moments, the parents and their two sons thoroughly enjoyed each other's sallies and antics.

Charles Herbert, the first addition to the family, was born November 22, 1869. Le Roy Ray, the younger boy, joined the group not quite seven years later — on October 26, 1876.

Dr. Walter L. Garrett, Mrs. Stoddard's nephew, recalled vividly an amusing scene which happened in the early 1880's at the Stoddard home at 36 Elm Street. The housekeeper, a much-enduring woman and the recipient of many practical jokes, was often on the verge of quitting. One day she made a large pie and put it on the kitchen windowsill to cool. Stoddard and his sons, who were rough-housing in the backyard, saw the pie and decided to subject the somewhat surly domestic to a further test of temperament.

After a short huddle the three went their separate ways — one of the boys removed the pie from its ledge, the other son returned with a large bit and bitstock, while the father was providing a can of gunpowder and a long fuse. The trio then made a great production out of boring a hole through the anticipatedly tough top crust of the pie, filling the fissure with black powder and inserting a five or six-foot fuse.

These noisy preliminaries to the main event attracted the attention of Mrs. Stoddard and the touchy cook. Sure of an audience the chief conspira-

tor, with much ado, lit the fuse and sauntered — while the sons scamper-
ed — to the shelter of the barn to await developments. These were not long
in coming and were most audibly satisfactory. While the three held their
ears and put on a convincing show of mock fright, the flame and the
powder finally met. Pieces of pie and chunks of pie plate flew in several
directions — followed shortly afterward by the departure of the harried
housekeeper.

Mrs. Stoddard must have been an unusual woman. This is made quite
clear by the obituary which her husband wrote for the Glens Falls *Times* of
October 29, 1906, the day following her death:

"Born January 21, 1850; entered into rest October 28, 1906.

"Like a tired child she fell asleep. Like the running down of a clock
a helpful life ended.

"It was her nature to do things for others. Her years were full of continued effort in which her own interests were but little considered. Her
later days were productive of lasting good.

"Her nature made possible the extremes. As a child it was alternate
sunshine and showers. She loved the sunshine best and was not made to
know in earlier days that the rain was necessary. She was impulsive and
never learned to hide her feelings. She espoused any cause that appealed
to her, without reasoning as to whether it was for her interests or against
them.

"Troubles that come into every condition were met defiantly by a
spirit that in earlier life had never been denied and always she rose above
disappointments — to a higher plane.

"Long-continued illness made her life for years one of pain and suffering, but with steady endurance she found comfort in the intervening hours
of rest and looked brightly forward to days of comfort that must surely
come.

"And come they did at last, when from a bed of sickness where all save
herself had despaired, saved for a time by the surgeon's knife, but seemingly as a wreck on a hopeless shore, she came under the new thought of
Christian Science and a new life opened before her. She absorbed the
truths of the new faith and with all the enthusiasm of her early youth put
into practice its precepts which, condensed, are told in one word — love.

"Once more her life was all sunshine. Those who came into close contact with her felt its cheery warmth, and once more with elastic step she
went about 'without an ache or a pain' as she many times averred. Acting
in accordance with her new belief, her life was devoted to its work, and
many declare that through her they found the light and by her ministra-
tions have come up out of sickness. The testimony of those who through
her have been healed are her jewels. Her sweeter flowers are tributes of
acknowledgement from those of other beliefs who have seen results and
stood convinced before her earnest purpose.

"In her church work she sought only the general good. She was willing to serve in any capacity where she could be effective and, to whatever position she was assigned, faithfully performed all that came to her to do. She loved her work among those who sought her help and pursued it with all the intentness of her nature. She planned great things and time and strength seemed her promise. For four years she rejoiced in her new condition; then, when many leaned on her, came signs of physical exhaustion. But when friends tried to make her take more thought for herself, she laughed at their warnings and insisted that strength would be given. It did seem, miraculously at times, when she would rise from a bed which, under the old thought, would have been called a bed of sickness, and go out to help others, returning exhausted yet smiling bravely to show that she had been equal to the demand.

"It is nearly two years since others began to see, yet she would make no admission. Her professed belief, backed by an indomitable spirit, would not let her admit weakness though physical failure made it plain. She would not yield but step by step fell back only when pressed beyond resistance. On each succeeding plane she held on as bravely and as resolutely to her way as though she had stood there from the first.

"Without pronounced disease she weakened steadily. Malnutrition is the verdict of those who see results without knowing causes. For the past year solid food has been a means of torture that could not be hidden. She made no complaint, but often would rise from the table and go away by herself so that others need not know. For a long time liquid food only could be given or retained. For nearly two months she was confined to her room, at times carried out into the sunshine that she so loved, but never a word of repining or to indicate that she anticipated anything but recovery for the continuance of her work. Any suggestion leading up to the thought that the end might be near met only silence that made words in others impossible. That she undoubtedly realized that she looked into the Unknown cannot be doubted. She seldom smiled and her expressed thoughts were of earnest things.

"A week ago there came a shock that left one side helpless and rendered speech difficult but, when asked how she felt, her reply was always 'Pretty good.' The spirit that prompted such words was the keynote of her life.

"She was sturdy friend to those she called friends. She saw good in everyone. No one knew her to speak evil of others unnecessarily. For human weaknesses she always found excuse. If no good could be said, she kept silent. After this, while seemingly indifferent to matters going on around, her hand that still had strength sought others continually and by a slight pressure answered questions asked. Then for a day she lay like one asleep until at last, gently sighing, like a tired child, the end came. The old smile that had been so long absent came back to her face."

Charles Herbert Stoddard, S. R.'s older son, was born in Glens Falls on November 22, 1869. While he was still in high school he enlisted in the

LeRoy and Charles Herbert Stoddard

Eighteenth Separate Company of the National Guard and thus started an outstanding military career. Entering Cornell University in 1889 he was made corporal and then sergeant in the cadet corps. The following year he received the warrants of first sergeant, and sergeant-major; in the spring of 1891 he was commissioned first lieutenant and adjutant. In the fall of that year he was promoted to captain; the next year he received his appointment as colonel, which rank he held until his graduation. During his junior and senior years he held the office of acting adjutant-general, the highest post in the corps of cadets.

In 1890 he was winner of the first prize in the competitive drill of that year. In 1891 and 1892 he served as commanding officer of a volunteer company composed of the military enthusiasts of the drill exhibitions against other such organizations. Upon graduation he was cited as the head of the list of college graduates eligible for commissions in the United States Army.

In 1894 he received his law degree from New York University and was admitted to the bar the same year. While practicing law in New York he still retained his interest in military affairs. In 1897 he obtained permission from Col. F. V. Greene, commander of the Seventy-first Regiment New

York National Guard, to organize another company to complete the regiment's quota of ten.

The noteworthy feature of this group was that its membership, by the specific request of Capt. Stoddard, was limited to college graduates. In explaining this rather unusual prerequisite, the organizer said: "College men, and especially fraternity men, possess an esprit de corps that you don't find in any other class of men. It is a natural result of college associations, engendered by the love of Alma Mater. I have a fine group of men and I expect to make Company E. the best company — barring none — in the National Guard within a year at the most."

After an intensive personal recruiting campaign, highlighted by a series of informal receptions which stressed the social advantages of membership, Capt. Stoddard selected 52 of his friends and sent engraved invitations to each. By unanimous vote Stoddard was elected by them to lead the collegians and did so during the first year of the Spanish-American War.

At the close of the war in Cuba Capt. Stoddard joined the Twenty-ninth New York Infantry and saw two years of active service in the Philippines (1899-1901) and during the Boxer Rebellion. Whenever and wherever he could he made a photographic record of his experiences. Of particular interest were those which caught the incidents in the jungle warfare, the camp life, the forced marches and the storming of the Filipino forts. When he returned home Stoddard used these pictures to illustrate a lecture program which included successful appearances at the Brooklyn Institute, the Glens Falls Opera House and before other audiences.

When the United States entered World War I Stoddard was promoted to full colonel and saw much action in France as the commander of the 315th Infantry Division.

After his return to civilian life he was one of the first lawyers to represent the Coca-Cola company. The author and publisher of law books he practiced his profession in Philadelphia, then in New York City for 26 years before moving to Massachusetts. He died on May 9, 1943 and was survived by his wife, Mrs. Ella Aldrich Stoddard.

LeRoy Ray, the younger son, was born in Glens Falls on October 26, 1876. Both he and his older brother made the most of the numerous advantages offered by a picturesque small town during the final decades of the nineteenth century. While his boyhood was for the most part pleasant and uneventful, one incident, as described by his father in a Glens Falls *Times* article dated November 24, 1890, must have lingered long in his memory:

The Gun Went Off

"Le Roy Stoddard and Ira Casavant went gunning Saturday. They are just common-sized boys and each has had fifteen years of varied earthly experience. They had been hunting together before and felt that it was no more than right for them to take a little wholesome recreation after five days of arduous mental labor under Supt. Williams at the Union School.

"They laid in a supply of four fat frankfurters at Vermilia's market, a long loaf of Vienna bread at the South End bakery and started for the Luzerne mountains. On the way out it occurred to them that they might get hungrier than they had at first thought, so they secured five more frankfurters at a market on West Street. Arrived at Goodspeedville and finding that the transportation of the provisions called for an outlay of muscular tissue that could only be replaced by food, they created some stir in commercial circles by the purchase of half a dozen red herrings, which they added to their supplies and started westward.

"They tramped the five miles to the foot of the mountain and there, in approved frontier style, built a campfire in a hollow by a rock and proceeded to feast on broiled frankfurters, toasted bread and red herring for dessert, all washed down by copious drafts of mountain water from a deserted tomato can picked up on the way.

"Dinner over, then came the business of the day. Chase was given to a red squirrel which ran chippering away to cover under an old stump. Ira was armed with a .22 calibre 'pocket rifle' with 12-inch barrel and a wire shoulder piece. Roy had a .44 calibre shotgun of the same general make. Roy planted himself like a youthful Colossus of Rhodes over the hole where the game had vanished, his gun pointed downward while Ira prodded around in various cavities. Suddenly he heard Roy's gun go Bang!

" 'Djugitem?' shouts Ira.

" 'I'm shot!' from Roy.

" 'You're foolin'!'

"But contrary to his usual habit Roy wasn't fooling. He slaps out a ring of fire that is enlarging a hole on the inside of his right trouser leg near the bottom, tears off the shoe and, with Ira's help, the stocking, thereby showing a black-mouthed opening in the inner side of his foot. There the charge had entered, striking just in front of the ankle bone and barely grazing the main bones of his foot. One or two pellets had passed entirely through to the bottom; the rest remained inside somewhere.

"The two boys bound their handkerchiefs tightly around the wounded foot and on three legs, like the three-legged man in the circus, went hopping down the mountainside to the house of a farmer. There they found a motherly woman who needed but an intimation of the trouble to set about doing the right thing at once. The wounded leg was soon in a tub of hot water and remained there while Ira went to a neighbor for horses and wagon to take them back to Glens Falls.

" 'You ought to be paid for all this,' said Roy, thinking regretfully that nearly all his money had gone for frankfurters and red herrings.

" 'Bless you, don't you s'pose your mother would do as much for my boy if he was in your place?' asked the kind-hearted woman, who saw only the need of help, such as she could give.

"The neighbor too, disdaining all idea of pay, came with his big wagon and horses, and with a lot of blankets and straw to make the injured member as comfortable as possible on the trip to the village.

"It took Dr. Phelps more than an hour to do the job to his satisfaction, as he had to lay open the wound right to the bottom of the foot, following the course of the charge. Then he had to probe about and cut off the ragged burned edges and pick out the shot — more than a hundred of them — along with pieces of trousers, bits of elastic and other things the blast had carried in. All the while this was going on Roy played on his new Pomperian ocarina to divert his mind from what the doctor was doing. This, with the very best intentions, was only a partial success as occasional false notes, contorted body and cold sweat testified; but the doctor, at the end of the operation said that his patient was a 'brick,' which is considered a good, square, solid compliment.

"Roy now occupies a brand-new two-dollar woven wire cot in the corner of the second-best room in the house. There he receives his friends and compares notes with fellow sufferers; at intervals of about twenty minutes, night and day, has applications of hot cloths as the present result of his adventure. As a further result he will not attend school for some time, but it is thought that no serious permanent trouble will follow.

"Moral for *boys:* When you go gunning take all the frankfurters, bread, herrings and almost anything you want — but leave the gun at home.

"Moral for *fathers:* If your boy asks to go hunting, before he has won at least three marksman's bars by practice on the 18th Separate Company's range under Capt. Garrett — take a strap to him.

"Moral for *mothers:* Mothers, — God bless them — don't need any moral. They are right in their motherly instinct every time."

After graduation from Glens Falls Academy Le Roy entered New York University and in due time completed his medical course. After his internship he was appointed house physician of Saks & Co., a leading New York City store. On a trip to the Midwest Dr. Stoddard met Carolyn Williams of Detroit, an accomplished vocalist, who later went to New York to continue her musical training. The two were married on March 14, 1906 in the Little Church Around the Corner.

It is not known whether this marriage was terminated by death or divorce but it is known that Dr. Stoddard's second wife was Alice Nielson, the singing star of several of Victor Herbert's light operas, and former head soprano of the Boston Opera Company. The doctor had reputedly fallen in love with her the first time he had seen her on the stage. They were married in 1917 and divorced a few years later.

When S. R. Stoddard died, in 1917, she sang at a benefit performance which was held at the Glens Falls Opera House. She died in a New York nursing home on March 9, 1943 and since she was practically penniless, her funeral expenses were paid by a friend.

Dr. Stoddard specialized in plastic surgery and became prominent in that field both here and abroad. While getting further training in this aspect of surgery in France many of his cases were war casualties. Most of his cosmetic patients in the United States were wealthy women and female stars of the entertainment world.

Dr. Stoddard's third wife was Mrs. Vince Booth Hubbell of New York City. They were married in July, 1940.

During the evening of March 18, 1943 Dr. Stoddard was found dead in his room in the Emerson Hotel in Baltimore, Maryland.

Complying with previous instructions his brother Charles scattered Le Roy's ashes over the Hudson River.

Seneca Ray Stoddard's second wife was Emily Doty, whom he married in 1907. She died in 1936 and was buried near S. R. in the Pine View Cemetery Glens Falls.

Chapter 15

The Final Years

Although it should be evident by now that S. R. Stoddard made his mark as a guidebook writer, mapmaker, lecturer, author and editor, his most memorable and enduring works were his camera masterpieces. So outstanding were they that they won for him comparable ranking with two other great 19th century photographers — William H. Jackson and Mathew Brady. Noteworthy, too, all three of these gifted men, pioneers in their craft, were born within sight of the Adirondacks—Stoddard in Wilton, Jackson in Peru and Brady near Lake George.

While it has never been settled for certain whether it was Brady or his numerous assistants who deserve the credit for recording photographically the triumphs and tribulations of the Civil War, there is no uncertainty whatsoever about Jackson's wonderful Western photos and Stoddard's less well-known but effective film records of the West as well as the Adirondacks and other areas.

Jackson also used water colors and pencil with considerable skill. So did Stoddard even though he did not actively exploit this ability. The latter's Lake George drawings indicate sensitivity and skill in that medium. Other painting, especially the large signed vista of Keene Valley from Prospect Hill, dated 1877, and several smaller studies of that lovely valley and the impressive Indian Pass from Summit Rock show equal ability.

Furthermore, his painstakingly tinted photographs were art creations in themselves. These were popular and sold well for relatively high prices to such individuals as William West Durant, Henry van Hoevenbergh and other collectors.

Stoddard's artistic ability was well recognized by his fellow citizens in Glens Falls and Warren County. In 1908 and again in 1913 he was art editor and photographer for the folio-sized souvenir publications extolling the considerable charms, assets and history of town and county. The first of these descriptive and illustrative editions required a year of preparation and the careful study of nearly two hundred books of a similar type from foreign as well as American sources.

Entitled "Glens Falls, the Empire City," the cover, drawn by Stoddard, was an eye-catching montage depicting the era of the Indian, Munro's surrender to Montcalm at nearby Lake George in 1757, Abercrombie's mighty host on their way to Ticonderoga and disaster in 1758, the building of Fort Amherst in 1762, a Quaker form, a view of the Falls through a bridge arch and the flag-draped town hall. Dedicated to Charles Evans Hughes, Glens Falls native, governor and later Chief Justice of the Supreme Court, the volume also contained a history of the town, written by James A. Holden, biographies of its most illustrious residents and sixty-five pages of Stoddard photographs — a total of 768 separate pictures in addition to accompanying and appropriate background and border designs.

The second similar project, that of 1913, marked the Warren County Centennial Celebration. This issue also featured a Stoddard cover design showing vignettes of history from wilderness days to the present: the red deer, the red man, the white hunter, the pioneer and the business man. Progress in transportation was symbolized by the horse-drawn wagon, the canal boat, the trolley, the autobus and the open touring car of that period. This commemorative issue contained historical accounts of varying lengths covering Warren County and its twelve townships. Most of this was undoubtedly written by James A. Holden, State Historian and Glens Falls resident. Also included in this thirty-eight page publication were memorial biographies of the most prominent deceased Glens Falls residents and a lengthy list of those who had formerly lived in the county.

As explained by Addison B. Colvin, the Centennial Celebration chairman, the object of the event was to bring to the attention of all those who might be interested the prominence of the county, its advantages and beauties.

To Stoddard belongs much of the credit for making those inducements visible because the views, individual and group pictures — 366 in all — were taken and arranged by him. This labor occupied most of a year and netted very little money because he considered it to be an opportunity for public service. It also represented the last major effort of his career.

Besides his paintings, tinted photographs and cover drawings S. R. Stoddard also excelled in sketches of people and places. These he used as illustrations for the guidebooks, in articles for his *Northern Monthly* and in both his books on foreign travel — *The Cruise of the Friesland* and *The Midnight Sun*. Other examples of his clever use of this form of art appear frequently in his unpublished manuscripts — particularly in the two-volume *Cruise of the Atlantis.*

His artistic as well as his literary ability also found expression and profit in the production of advertising brochures for hotels, railroads and land development firms. In most instances he took the pictures, wrote the copy, designed the booklet and arranged for the printing. Some of these brochures, especially those for the Fort William Henry and Crosbyside Hotels at Lake George, the Lake Placid Club and the Under-Cliff at Lake

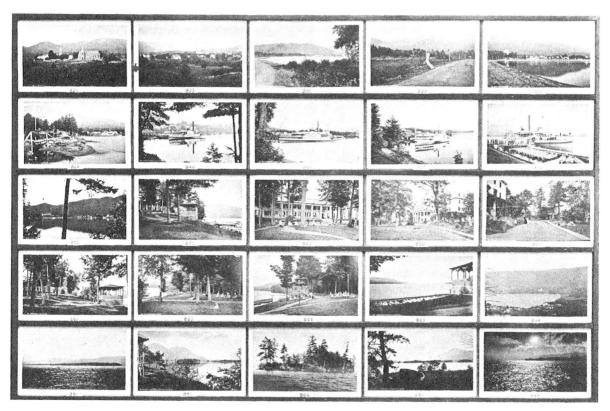

Caldwell, Crosbyside (Lake George)

165

Developing Studio

Placid, the Raquette Lake Hotel, The Westport Inn on Lake Champlain and the Taylor House at Schroon Lake were rather elaborate.

Among other hotels which used his booklets were the Windsor and the Mansion Houses at Elizabethtown; St. Hubert's and the Mount Porter House at Keene Valley; Childwold Park House at Lake Massawepie; the Lake Harris House; the Wayside Inn at Newcomb; Kellogg's Lake House and the Sagamore at Long Lake; Whiteface Inn and Stevens House at Lake Placid; the Algonquin, Ampersand and Wawbeek at Saranac Lake; the Cascade House; the Antlers, Hemlocks, Brightside and Hunter's Rest at Raquette Lake; Blue Mountain House and the Prospect House at Blue Mountain Lake; Bald Mountain House, Eagle Bay Hotel and Camp Neodak on the Fulton Chain and Ralph's on Upper Chateaugay Lake.

The Lake George clients were the Grove Point House, Hotel Willard, Hotel Uncas, Trout House, Trout Pavilion, Silver Bay House, Sabbath Day Point Hotel, Rising House, the Lake House, the Sagamore, the Algonquin, Horicon Lodge and Hulett House.

For the railroad trade Stoddard published a booklet for the Central Vermont R. R. and supplied most of the photographs for the Delaware and Hudson and the Adirondack Railway advertising literature.

Besides the brochures, albums and photographs which were sold at the various mountain resorts, Stoddard also had a full line of postcards, colored and black and white.

Another source of income for the incredibly industrious photographer was the sale of colored slides to various schools, institutions and other lecturers. In one year alone — 1896 — the Museum of Natural History in New York City ordered more than 5,000 for resale.

Somehow during his busy career Stoddard twice found time to become an inventor: on May 22, 1882 he obtained a patent on a combination photographic plate and film holder; on March 14, 1905 he patented a new and improved electric trolley. He also improved and designed many of the cameras which he used.

The Stoddard holder consisted of two parts — a light, single wooden plate holder including the focusing screen, which was permanently fastened to the camera; and thin metal individual shields for protecting the sensitive glass plates (pressed paper shields for films) which were put into the holder for exposure. The Stoddard holder was attached to the camera by removing the ground glass provided with the camera and screwing it (the holder) fast in the place usually occupied by the plate holder. When the holder was closed for focusing, the ground glass was held in position by four springs. When the focus had been adjusted, the holder was opened, the shield containing the dry plate or film was put in and the holder closed, locked securely in place by the spring catches. The slide was then drawn and a shutter in the holder closed the slit making the camera ready for action.

By using this combination plate and film holder fourteen plates or two dozen films could be packed into a space only *three inches thick.* A great improvement over the earlier, bulkier equipment.

The device, which featured cheapness of production, economy of space, safety and convenience, was manufactured and marketed by E. L. Elliot Co., of Auburn, N. Y.

According to the patent description the electrical trolleys, as developed by S. R. Stoddard, could be put to general use but were primarily effective in connection with so-called "third-rail systems." The device itself seems quite complicated and it is not known whether or not it was ever exploited. However, it does indicate still another facet of the inventor's versatility.

Even though his photographic work, his lecture trips, travels, map and guidebook business accounted for much of his time, Stoddard nevertheless did not neglect a different interest — that of temperance. He was very active as a member and leader in the Billy J. Clark division of the Sons of Temperance. As the first society ever formed to have as its goal total abstinence, it grew to the point where it had nearly two million members in the United States as well as many branch organizations in England, Ireland and Australia. Besides being a frequent delegate to many of the state conventions, Stoddard was also, in 1891, nominated for member of the Assembly by the Warren County Prohibition party. Although his party waged a spirited battle at the polls, it was not strong enough numerically to elect any of its candidates.

It is noteworthy that in 1872 Stoddard was commissioned to paint the portraits of Dr. Billy J. Clark and James Mott, the Temperance Society's founders. In due time these likenesses were completed and placed in the meeting room.

While Stoddard's correspondence reveals that he attracted and retained many friends during his lifetime, probably his closest friend was Wallace Bruce, who was a poet, author of *The Hudson,* an excellent prose work; a lecturer and the U. S. Consul at Edinburgh. Their paths had often crossed on lecture tours and several times they had appeared on the same program or during the same lecture series sponsored by the Winter Chautauqua at De Funiak Springs, Florida. In December 1889, while Bruce was in Scotland this poetry exchange occurred:

> My dear Stoddard:
> Though seas are wide
> That roll between —
> Your bill is spied
> As will be seen;
> The face is met
> With check you see
> And hope to get

                    Receipt from thee.
                         Respectfully
                    and punctually
                         W. BRUCE

Reply:
          Dear Bruce:
               Your words from o'er the sea
          Come like a benison to me.
               So legal tender, yet so terse —
          You never wrote more touching verse.
               The scroll that bears the hero's name
          Traced by the hand that wrought his fame,
               I value high but more by half
          The scrap that bears thy autograph.
               Cause why? It pays in full to date
          My bill for forty-two nought eight
               Oh were it more! Oh, happiness
          Enough!
                         Yours ever,
                         S. R. S.

A study of his ledgers and account books reveals that during his lifetime Stoddard grossed a considerable amount of money but never became wealthy. Obviously such ventures also involved sizable expenditures for supplies, travel costs and wages to his employees. On his photographing trips he was usually accompanied by Oblenis, his brother-in-law, and occasionally by Frank, his brother. Stoddard seldom hired more than two guides and, more often than not only one, in order to keep the overhead as low as possible. Usually he had two or three women helping in processing the prints, assembling the albums and taking care of the orders.

In spite of shrewd business methods by his numerous advertising arrangements with various means of public transportation on his many trips — to help cover expenses — Stoddard apparently had to work hard to meet financial obligations and provide a good living for his family. Obviously, the expensive education of his two sons was no minor concern and this responsibility continued until 1908, when Le Roy had started his medical practice. Such an overhead understandably left very little for the aging father's declining years.

Not much is known about Stoddard's life during the interval from 1912-1915. The guidebook and map revisions were published and the photography business continued. Part of 1912 and most of 1913 were devoted to his duties as art editor of the Warren County Centennial souvenir program but after that the curtain started to close.

The obituary which was printed in the Glens Falls *Post-Star* on Friday, April 27, 1917 gives this explanation: "Mr. Stoddard's illness dates back more than two years, at which time forces appeared to be more mental than physical. Up to a year ago an indomitable spirit refused to admit weakness though physical failure made it plain. Since late last Fall Mr. Stoddard had been confined to his home and to his bed since Christmas. He fought valiantly through all the successive stages of his physical decline, until at last, like a clock running down he gave up and gently, peacefully fell into the long sleep."

The cause of his death was arteriosclerosis.

The *Post-Star* writer, who knew him well, added these comments: "Mr. Stoddard was a sturdy friend to those he called friends. He saw only the good in people and always remained silent if this could not be expressed. Thoroughly unselfish he lived, while gentleness appeared to govern his conduct throughout his life, and right to the end it appeared to control his advent to the Great Beyond."

Another tribute to S. R. Stoddard may be found in the biographical volume of Dr. James Sullivan's *History of New York State* (1523-1927). The author states: "It would be impossible to overestimate the value of Mr. Stoddard's work in the education of the American people. In a day when textbooks in schools were sparsely illustrated, when the geography was the source of all the information a child had about the world he lived in outside his immediate circle, the stereopticon views, the books, the magazine articles of Mr. Stoddard, all delightfully illustrated and often in color taught Americans young and old just how the world looked. Nor does this outstanding achievement obscure Mr. Stoddard's goodness, strength of character, and sweetness of temper. His friends and his family reaped the happy benefit of these qualities. He was a man of men."

While he was still alive and could therefore appreciate such praise an editor wrote these words in the New York *Mail and Express* of June 9, 1894: "Close upon the heels of Murray came S. R. Stoddard with his camera, his notebook and his brush, all of which he used continuously to make the fame of the Adirondack Wilderness known to the outside world. Stoddard has done even more than Murray to publish the results of his discoveries for in guidebooks, on his maps, on the lecture platform, on the screen, in poetry and in song, he has for more than a quarter of a century preached the Adirondacks and them glorified."

A present-day evaluation of Stoddard's place in history was expressed in the June-July, 1949 issue of *The Conservationist*: "Any of a dozen appellations would describe Seneca Ray Stoddard but posterity will know him best as the man who, with his bulky, old-fashioned camera and tripod, his glass plates and emulsions captured the Adirondacks. By recording so faithfully and with such feeling the beauty of the North Woods, Stoddard provided a powerful argument for both their protection and their enjoyment. He was a conservationist."

Those apt words sum up the remarkable career of the versatile, incredibly industrious man from Glens Falls.

Stoddard trademark

Appendix

Account of the *Atlantis* cruise which was printed in the St. John, New Brunswick *Globe* (August 5, 1886)

ADVENTUROUS VOYAGERS

One of the smallest, if not the smallest, craft that has ever made the voyage from New York to St. John arrived in port this forenoon on the steamer "Cumberland." Some three years ago S. R. Stoddard, publisher, of Glens Falls, N. Y., and his companion, R. B. Burchard, editor of the *American Canoeist* sailed from that town in the canoe "Atlantis." This trip down the Hudson River and through the Sound was relatively un-eventful but outside of Provincetown, Mass., some boisterous weather was encountered and the boat capsized. After righting the "Atlantis" a half dozen times it was found impossible to keep her on her keel. During the ordeal some of the rigging and sails were lost but fortunately a pilot boat came to their aid and they were taken in to port.

The next season, the craft was refitted and put in trim again, the two adventurers sailed her as far as Woods Hole and thence to Bar Harbor, where she was laid up until this year. On Sunday last they resumed the trip and put in that night at Beaubois Island. She then touched at Libby Island, Sailor's Cove and Pisarinco, remaining overnight at each place. . .

From here (St. John) they intend to sail up the Bay to Wolfe River and thence over to Truro.

The "Atlantis" is 18 feet long, has a 36 inch beam, is 18 inches deep and draws only 8 inches of water. The hull is built of cedar and the deck of spruce and butternut in strips one inch wide running lengthwise. She has two masts, which can be unshipped at will, and is also furnished with a mainsail, foresail and jib. The mountings are of brass and all her fittings and gear are of the miniature kind but very strong. The blocks are not over an inch and a half long and nickel-plated. Her rudder and center-board are made in such a manner that in shallow water or when they hit an obstruction they fold up.

She has watertight compartments in the bow and stern, a pair of air pumps, two outrigged oarlocks, oars and paddles. A gasoline stove is hung in the middle of the boat so designed that it stays in position whatever way the canoe is pitching.

The sail arrangement and material, developed by Mr. Stoddard, are a combination of the lateen and the ordinary lug sail and combine the good qualities of each. They can be readily reefed or the reefs shaken out by the pull of a rope.

From the forepeak she flies an American Canoe Association burgee, of which club they are members. Altogether the "Atlantis" is a magnificent-looking craft.

Upon their arrival here the travelers stated that the "Cumberland" is a fine boat, that she has as fine a set of officers and men as they have ever seen and that the cuisine is excellent. From Truro, their destination on this final phase of the trip, Messrs. Stoddard and Burchard will go by rail to Moncton and then, after spending a few days, will come back to St. John. From here they will start on their homeward journey.

Adirondack Miscellany

Lower Edmond's Pond (Cascade Lake)

Upper Edmond's Pond

173

Lake Trout Upper Saranac Lake

Bartlett's, Saranac Lake

Upper Jay, Essex County

Upper Ausable Pond — Saddleback

175

Ausable Pass from Beede House

Keene Valley from Prospect Hill

Upper Ausable Pond

Upper Ausable Pond

Root's Hotel, Adirondacks

Echo Camp, Raquette Lake

Long Lake, Sagamore Hotel

Long Lake, West from Sagamore

179

Tupper Lake, McClure's

North from Grand View, Lake Placid

Lake Placid House, Adirondacks

Hulett's Landing, Lake George

Composite: Schroon Lake

Composite: Luzerne

Trudeau Sanitarium patient snowshoers

Horican Sketching Club, 1882

Adirondack Lumber Camp

Adirondack Lumber Shanty

184

Tollgate, French Mountain (Lake George)

"Homeward Bound" — Lake George 1879

185

Index